Labor Market Dynamics in Libya

A WORLD BANK STUDY

Labor Market Dynamics in Libya

Reintegration for Recovery

WORLD BANK GROUP

Contents

Boxes

Figures

Map

Tables

Acknowledgments

This policy note was developed as part of the World Bank's Libya Employment and Skills Technical Assistance Program. The authors extend their gratitude to technical representatives from various public authorities for their hospitality and coordination as part of this work, notably the Ministry of Planning, the Ministry of Labor, and the Bureau of Statistics and Census.

The World Bank team comprised Heba Elgazzar (Senior Economist, Human Development), Caroline Bahnson (Social Development Specialist), Pietro Calice (Senior Private Sector Development Specialist), Nada Choueri (Lead Country Economist, Libya), Erik Churchill (Communications Specialist), Eric Davin (Labor Assessment Consultant), Laurence Hargreaves (Labor Assessment Consultant), Khalid El Massnaoui (Senior Economist, Poverty Reduction and Economic Management), Abdel Rahman Lahga (Assistant Professor of Economics, University of Tunis, Labor Consultant), Francesca Recanatini (Senior Economist, Public Sector), Paola Ridolfi (Senior Country Officer, Maghreb), and Manal Quota (Education Specialist). The work benefited from helpful discussions with Kamel Braham (Lead Education Specialist, Human Development), Joelle Businger (Country Program Coordinator, Maghreb), Fabrice Houdart (Senior Country Officer, Maghreb), Maria Laura Sanchez Puerta (Senior Economist, Social Protection and Labor), David Robalino (Manager and Lead Economist, Jobs), Friederike Rother (Senior Operations Officer, Social Protection and Labor), and Alexandria Valerio (Senior Economist, Education). The report benefited from helpful editing by Alicia Hetzner (Senior Editorial Consultant) as well as Abdia Mohamed and Rick Ludwick (World Bank) for excellent publishing support.

The team sincerely thanks the peer reviewers for their useful feedback and comments: Ghazala Mansuri (Lead Economist, Development Research Group), David Newhouse (Senior Economist, Poverty Reduction and Economic Management, South Asia), Lawrence Orr (Professor of Economics, Johns Hopkins University), and Michel Welmond (Lead Education Specialist, Human Development, East Asia and Pacific). The team is also grateful for the to support provided by Patrick Biribonwa (Program Assistant), Hend Irhiam (Operations Analyst), Abdurrahman Karwa (Program Assistant), Francoise Mukamana (Program Assistant), Mark Reading (Security Officer, Country Operations), and Besma Saidi Refai (Program Assistant). The team appreciates the valuable counsel provided by Yasser El-Gammal (Sector Manager, Social Protection and Labor) and Marouane El-Abassi (Resident Representative, Libya), and the overall guidance of Simon Gray (Country Director, Maghreb).

The team is indebted to helpful consultations with representatives from private sector firms and civil society organizations in Libya, particularly the Tripoli Chamber of Commerce, Tawakkel Libya Foundation for Development, Hope Foundation, and Global Shapers, as well as international organizations including the European Union, United Nations Support Mission in Libya (UNSMIL), United Kingdom Department for International Development (DfID), and the Danish Cooperation.

Executive Summary

Introduction

Since the 2011 uprising that toppled the former regime, Libya has been mired in deep political strife. Today, limited opportunities exist for reintegrating youth and ex-combatants into the labor market.

For the four decades preceding its 2011 uprising, Libya's already fragile post-independence institutions had been all but eradicated in name. An economy in which agriculture once flourished was converted wholesale to an oil-based rentier state of the most extreme kind. State monies were spent liberally on an inflating, nonperforming civil service and transfers. Energy, food, and in-kind subsidies of housing and living allowances gradually rose to exponential proportions, dwarfing those of other countries in the region.[1] In 2013, state subsidies comprised 14 percent of gross domestic product (GDP), accompanied by a doubling of the public wage bill relative to pre-uprising estimates to 17 percent of GDP (IMF 2013).[2]

Following the immediate post-revolution oil-consumption boom, in 2014 Libya's economy is in recession. Security is the greatest challenge to stability (World Bank 2014).[3] In 2003, the latest year for which official data are available, the poverty rate was estimated at 11.8 percent. Due to the ongoing conflict, rising unemployment, and increasingly weak public services, the poor and near-poor in Libya increasingly are at risk. When Libya suddenly found itself free of a notorious regime in October 2011, its public financial system could hardly function. At that time, there was much that remained to be rebuilt. Institutions, information,[4] and a modern public administration, which Libya had not seen in 40 years, had yet to be created.

Objectives of This Report

The objectives of this policy note are to (1) provide an initial assessment of Libya's labor market and (2) discuss policy options for promoting employability as part of a broader jobs strategy.

This assessment is based on a framework of the demand and supply for jobs in fragile contexts.[5] Shifting Libya from a rentier state to a diversified, productive economy through economic and technical partnerships would help to accelerate creating economic opportunities and jobs. In this sense, coalition building between public and private actors also would be a core tenet of state-building in Libya.

Main Findings

The vast majority (85 percent) of Libya's active labor force is employed in the public sector, a high rate even by regional standards. The rate for women is even higher (93 percent).

Prior to the uprising, in a population of 6 million, Libya's labor force comprised 2.6 million workers, nearly 50 percent of who were foreign. During the uprising, an estimated 1 million foreign laborers fled Libya. Based on 2012 data,[6] the country's labor force today stands at an estimated 1.9 million in a remaining population of approximately 5 million. Only 34 percent of the employed labor force is women.

In the active labor force, 1.5 million workers are employed in Libya. Whereas public sector employment accounts for the majority of activity, employment in industry (largely the oil sector) and agriculture accounts for only 10 percent of the labor force. This share is only 20 percent of the level seen nearly 30 years ago. Given the dominance of the public sector as the main employer, job security is high, particularly for 45-year-olds and above, who tend to have open-ended contracts. While nearly all public sector workers are covered by some form of social insurance, only 46 percent of private sector workers are enrolled—a striking difference. Wages in Libya are buttressed by substantive state subsidies on fuel and food, and social benefits for maternity, dependents, and the aging.

Libya has one of the highest unemployment rates in the world, particularly given its high rate of tertiary enrollment.

Overall unemployment increased from 13.5 percent in 2010 prior to the uprising to 19 percent in 2012 (figure ES.1). Youth unemployment is approximately 48 percent and female unemployment 25 percent. Given the inflated public sector, these patterns likely reflect, first and foremost, (a) a lack of private sector jobs for both unskilled and skilled Libyans. Additional contributors to unemployment are (b) inefficient school-to-work transitions; (c) job queuing for public sector jobs; (d) and a lower willingness for Libyans to accept jobs in trades and manual work, which, as a result, often are filled by low-skilled foreign workers. Jobs that are highly skilled also are filled by non-nationals. Thirty percent of firms have reported difficulty in recruiting qualified Libyan nationals.[7] The current report also found that firms recruit Libyan staff to meet labor regulation quotas while hiring foreign workers at various skill levels to fill actual business needs. For hiring, firms also tended give more weight to prior work experience than to educational background. This pattern suggests that labor market programs should be designed to more directly build job-relevant skills.

Jobseekers in Libya fall into different profiles. Only 15–30 percent of Libya's labor force is relatively skilled and likely could be hired readily if given access to

Figure ES.1 Unemployment Rate in Libya

percent

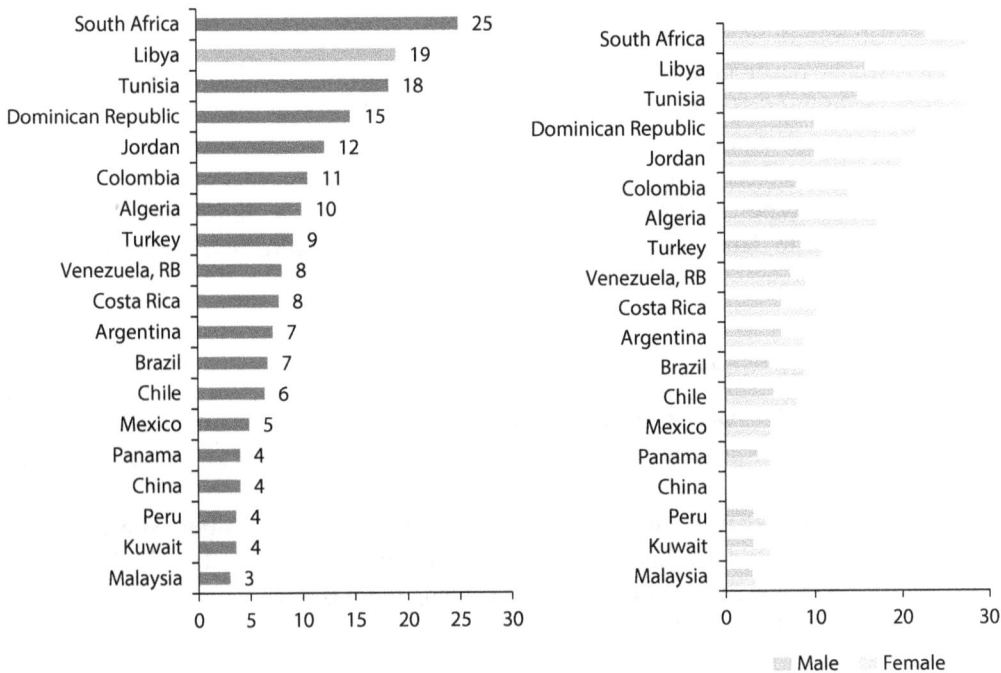

	Male	Female

Source: World Bank staff calculations; Libya LFS 2012 data; World Development Indicators (WDI) and International Labor Organization Key Indicators of the Labour Market (ILO KILM) database 2013.

basic job training and job search assistance. For the remainder of the unemployed work force, targeted interventions would need to be designed for advanced skills development, vocational training, reconversion, and apprenticeship and entrepreneurship programs. Ultimately, however, Libya's private sector would need to generate significantly more jobs in untapped sectors to absorb new entrants into the labor market.

Once the security situation stabilizes, investment climate reforms will be needed to accelerate growth and compensate for losses to job creation incurred as a result of recurring conflict.

Libya will need to establish a viable financial sector and widely improve access to credit, significantly simplify business regulations, and create strong incentives for investment in new sectors. Based on an analysis of firms' perspectives, the infrastructure, trade, hospitality, and agriculture sectors in the short to medium terms, and services and manufacturing in the long term, are expected to create the most jobs. Based on interviews conducted as part of the 2012 rapid assessment for this report, security concerns notwithstanding, firms had predicted approximately 6 percent growth over the coming two years. However, preliminary estimates suggest that growth will need to double this level to readily absorb job seekers.

Prior to the recent conflict in 2014, Libya had initiated a process to reform labor legislation. As a result of the political strife during 2014, the labor legislation reform process has stalled. To stimulate job creation in the private sector, labor reforms should be married with broader social protection reforms. Reforms will be needed to restructure civil service employment, address the quota system for hiring nationals versus non-nationals, and streamline and rationalize regulations regarding the types of hiring contracts. Social security coverage is weak in the private sector, in which only 46 percent of employees are covered. More analysis is necessary to evaluate the benefits structure, sustainability, and the cost of labor to determine how best to strengthen social protection while stimulating job creation.

Key Challenges

Libya's jobs challenge is compounded by historically weak institutions, a hampered private sector diversification and growth, and a mismatch of skills and labor market needs.

Still emerging from its revolution, Libya is mired in a transition whose fragility is exacerbated by underemployment and unemployment. In addition to an unstable political environment and ongoing periods of conflict, the biggest challenges facing the labor market are:

- **Access to finance and incentives in the business climate.** The weak business climate reduces labor force demand by not providing small, medium, and large enterprises with adequate access to finance, business services, and incentives to invest in emerging sectors such as construction, trade, services, and agribusiness.
- **Public sector as employer of choice.** The dominance of state-owned enterprises (SOEs) in the economy and the structure of civil service benefits reduce incentives to seek employment in the private sector.
- **Labor regulations regarding contracts, migration1, and hiring and firing.** Deterrent labor regulations governing the structure of contracts, quotas for nationals, training requirements, and hiring and firing procedures may limit, rather than promote, job creation.
- **Dichotomy of social security between the public and private sectors.** Low social insurance coverage in the private sector tends to increase queuing for public sector jobs.
- **Job-relevant skills, both high and low.** Firms face challenges in recruiting qualified nationals for both highly and low-skilled jobs.
- **Pre-graduate support for job placement.** Despite high tertiary enrollment, weak school-to-work transitions result in one of the world's highest youth unemployment rates.

Policy Options for the Short to Long Term

An integrated jobs strategy would help promote reintegration during Libya's transition phase and pave the way to boost employment in the long term.

This policy note highlighted multiple structural factors that affect the Libya's labor market, notably a nascent business climate and an unexperienced labor force. Mired in political instability, Libya faces challenges to youth and ex-combatant employment that can impact long-term stabilization and state-building. Given Libya's context, two key policy objectives emerge:

- **To build the fundamentals for sustainable, diversified growth.** Growth requires interventions to restore security and stable institutions, a well-functioning financial market, and a competitive investment climate over the long run.
- **To improve the efficiency of labor market insertion.** The lack of efficiency calls for interventions for youth and ex-combatants in the short run, such as through public-private partnerships (PPPs) for on-the-job training, followed by more structural reforms to labor policies and social protection in the public and private sectors.

To promote jobs and reintegration, an integrated jobs strategy is needed to tackle these dual objectives in three main policy areas (figure ES.2).

Figure ES.2   Policy Pathway to Jobs and Reintegration for Libya

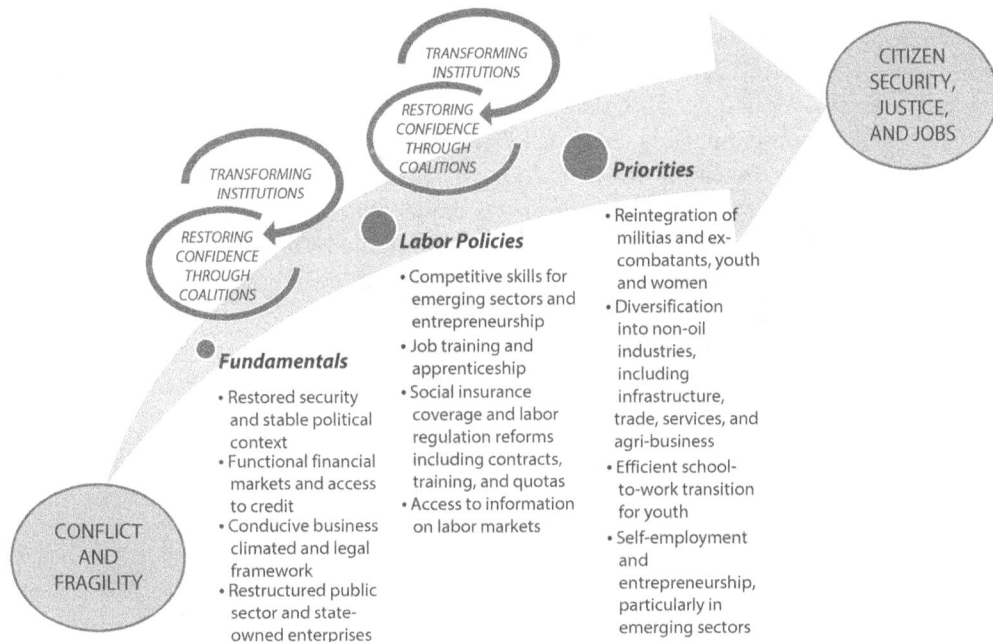

Source: World Bank staff.

These key reforms and interventions include:

- **Strengthening the stability and incentives within the business climate in the short to medium term,** particularly by boosting access to finance, business services, and incentives to invest in emerging sectors for small, medium, and large enterprises, particularly in sectors with a high job-creating potential in Libya such as construction, trade, services, and agribusiness
- **Shifting the role of the public sector as employer of choice in the medium term** by reducing the dominance in the economy of the public sector and state-owned enterprises
- **Ensuring labor regulations that guarantee adequate incentives for job creation in the private sector in the medium term,** notably in the structure of employment and training contracts, quotas for nationals and non-nationals, training requirements, and hiring and firing policies
- **Reducing the dichotomy of social security policies between the public and private sectors in the short to medium term,** particularly the low social insurance coverage in the private sector and queuing for public sector jobs
- **Targeting job-relevant skills development in the short to long term,** which will help reduce barriers faced by firms in recruiting qualified nationals for both high- and low-skilled jobs
- **Improving the school-to-work transition in the medium term** to facilitate labor market insertion among youth and women, especially given Libya's particularly high tertiary enrolment.

Moving forward, the realization of a jobs strategy that is based on Libya's economic vision will be needed. The strategy would need to address the range of challenges to Libya's business climate, labor market institutions, and educational system. For untapped sectors such as trade, services, tourism, and agribusiness, the potential is particularly great. As Libya's transition unfolds, building coalitions for improving the employment outlook will help support long-term state-building. Libya's challenges are in some respects similar to those faced by the rest of Middle East and North Africa as well as other middle-income and fragile contexts. However, Libya needs to both fill a long-standing, deep institutional vacuum *and* facilitate reconciliation among rival factions in a nascent state. Significant structural and institutional reforms are needed. Innovative public-private collaboration is already emerging in Libya that can pave the way for these reforms. Coalition-building can therefore accelerate the pace of change needed for jobs and reintegration in Libya, laying the foundation for a stronger future for all Libyans.

Notes

1. World Bank, *Libya Economic Monitoring Note, Spring* (Washington, DC: World Bank, 2014).
2. International Monetary Fund (IMF), *Libya, 2013 Article IV Consultation.* IMF Country Report 13/150, Washington, DC (2013).

3. World Bank, *Libya Economic Monitoring Note*.

4. Statistical information and data in Libya are sparse, making the present analysis challenging.

5. World Bank, *World Development Report 2011: Conflict, Security, and Development* (Washington, DC World Bank, 2011) and World Bank, *World Development Report 2013: Jobs* (Washington, DC: World Bank, 2012).

6. World Bank staff and Libya Bureau of Statistics and Census calculations using most recent data, Libya 2012 Labor Force Survey, Bureau of Statistics and Census, Ministry of Planning, Tripoli.

7. World Bank, *Libya 2010 Investment Climate Assessment* (Washington, DC: World Bank, 2011).

Abbreviations

BSC	Bureau of Statistics and Census
CLB	Council of Libyan Businessmen
CoC	Chamber of Commerce
CV	curriculum vitae
DDR	disarmament, demobilization, and reintegration
DIME	Development Impact Evaluation
EDB	Economic Development Board
ESDF	Economic and Social Development Fund
GDP	gross domestic product
GPC	General Projects Committee
HIB	Housing and Investment Board
ICA	Investment Climate Assessment
ICMPD	International Centre for Migration Policy Development
IDI	In-depth interview
ILO	International Labour Organization
IT	information technology
KII	Key Informant Interview
KILM	Key Indicators of the Labour Market (ILO)
LFPR	labor force participation rate
LFS	Labor Force Survey
LIDCO	Libyan Investment and Development Firm
LYD	Libyan dinar
M&E	monitoring and evaluation
MFZC	Misratah Free Zone Firm
MOE	Ministry of Economy
MOL	Ministry of Labor and Manpower
MOP	Ministry of Planning
ODAC	Organization for Development of Administrative Centers
OECD	Organisation for Economic Co-Operation and Development

OTJ	on-the-job
PFM	public financial management
PIAAC	Program for the International Assessment of Adult Competencies
PIB	Privatization and Investment Board
PPP	public-private partnership
PROBECAT	*Programa de Becas de Capacitación para Trabajadores Desempleados*
SME	small and medium enterprise
SOE	state-owned enterprise
STEP	Skills toward Employment and Productivity
UNESCO	United Nations Educational, Scientific, and Cultural Organization
USAID	United States Agency for International Development
WAC	Warriors Affairs Commission
WDI	World Development Indicators
US$	United States dollar

CURRENCY EQUIVALENTS

(Exchange Rate Effective as of January 17, 2015)
1 LYD = 0.76 US$
1 US$ = 1.33 LYD

GOVERNMENT FISCAL YEAR

January 1–December 31

CHAPTER 1

Introduction

Objectives of the Study

As of 2015, in many ways, Libya finds itself in a post-uprising situation that was inevitable. Over the four decades preceding its 2011 uprising, the country's already-fragile post-independence institutions were all but eradicated in name. An economy in which agriculture once flourished was converted wholesale to an oil-based rentier state of the most extreme kind. State monies were spent liberally on an inflating, nonperforming civil service and transfers. Moreover, energy, food, and in-kind subsidies on housing and living allowances gradually rose to exponential proportions, dwarfing those of other countries in the region.[1] By 2013, state subsidies comprised 14 percent of gross domestic product, followed by a doubling of the public wage bill relative to pre-uprising estimates to 17 percent of gross domestic product (GDP).[2]

Following the immediate post-revolution oil-consumption boom, by 2014, Libya's economy is in recession. Security poses the greatest challenge to stability.[3] The 2013 budget, whose envelope was 66.8 billion LD, reflected a spending surge of 90 percent of government spending relative to 2012. Due to government delays in approving the budget and political indecision regarding the public investment portfolio, capital spending decreased by 80 percent from 26 percent of GDP in 2010 to only 5.5 percent in 2013. The year 2014 is likely to be another recession year due to a lagging hydrocarbon output, which will shrink GDP by 10 percent; and a 15 percent slow-down in nonoil growth driven largely by public and private consumption. When Libya found itself free of a notorious regime in October 2011, its public financial system could hardly function. Much remained to be rebuilt, but institutions, information,[4] and a modern public administration— the likes of which Libya had not seen in 40 years—had yet to be created.

Yet, the biggest challenges that have overshadowed these barriers to a smooth transition reared their heads only at the end of 2011: the question of employment and, more conspicuous, that of youth and combatants. Although only a fraction of the population of the Arab Republic of Egypt and with important trade links to Tunisia, Libya is a society that is divided along tribal and militia lines far surpassing what is seen to its east or west. Although a natural and perhaps necessary phase during transition, the political uncertainties mired in sectarian strife have reached epic proportions, paralyzing an otherwise forward-looking nation. The very freedom fighters to whom Libya's citizens and her diaspora owed their new lives soon would reveal one of the most complex political undercurrents facing a transition country in the Middle East and North Africa. The dual challenges of integrating youth and ex-combatants into productive lives, while creating a functional labor market in which to absorb them,[5] likely are the most salient barriers to a successful economic and political transition facing Libya today.

The objectives of this policy note are to provide an initial assessment of key labor market indicators and discuss policy options for promoting employability as part of developing a broader jobs strategy for Libya. This evaluation adopts a conceptual framework of supply and demand for jobs and reintegration in fragile, resource-rich contexts (figure 1.1). Two recent *World Development Reports*—*Conflict, Security, and Development*[6] and *Jobs*[7]—provide the basis for this framework. Through selected lenses, they examine the demand and supply for labor and the role of jobs as a *core tenet* of peace- and state-building. Barriers to good jobs are framed as a *three-layered challenge* and are central to move from fragility to stability. The first layer is the *fundamentals*, or putting in place the right macroeconomic and governance foundations. The second layer describes *labor policies*, which include labor legislation and related policies such as those pertaining to education and social security. Depending on how they are designed, these policies can affect

Figure 1.1   Framework for Jobs and Reintegration in Fragile Contexts

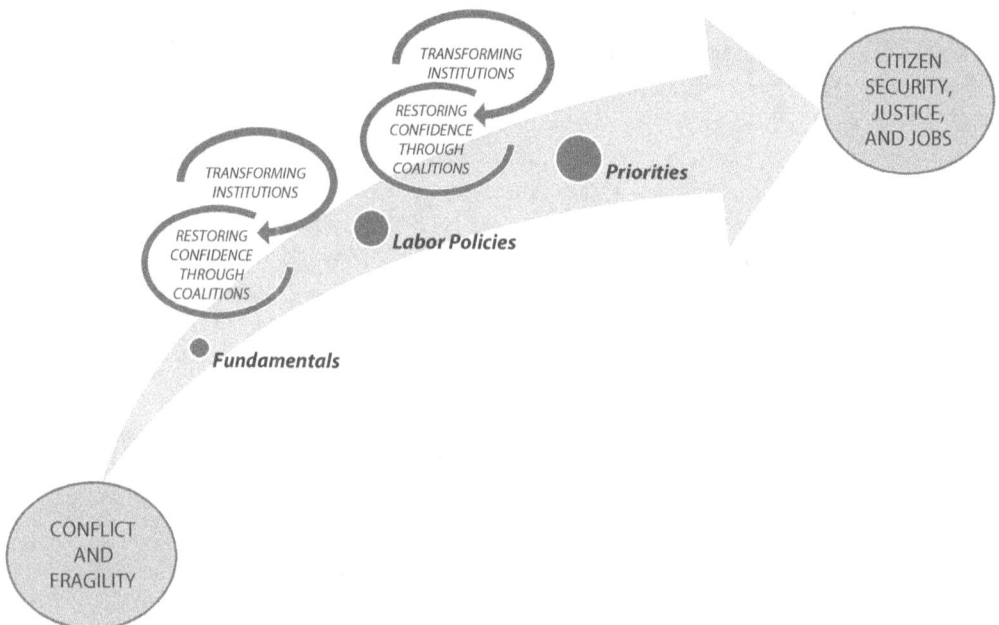

Source: Adapted from World Bank 2011 (6) and World Bank 2013 (7).

formal and informal job creation.[8] The third layer focuses on *priorities*, which further shape the policy agenda in terms of specific, critical development issues.

The analysis in the report was constrained by a lack of available data in Libya but was complemented by information collected through new tools for monitoring and evaluation. Primary data sources include the Libyan 2012 Labor Force Survey, conducted by the Libyan Bureau of Statistics and Census (BSC)[9]; and a qualitative evaluation of job seekers and firms conducted by the World Bank, the 2012 Rapid Labor Market Assessment. Administrative data from the Central Bank of Libya and the Warriors Affairs Commission (WAC) were used to analyze key economic indicators and labor force statistics related to ex-combatants, respectively.

As the rest of the report highlights, in Libya's case, the biggest challenges facing the transition and the labor market center on weak fundamentals. Affecting the demand for and supply of labor, they are:

- *Weak rule of law and political instability, including weak institutions*
- *Lack of an enabling business environment, including the financial market*
- *Lagging human capital, as indicated by high unemployment and educational indicators.*

Private and civil society actors are critical to supporting and implementing any public policy to boost employment in the short to medium term in contexts such as Libya, in which state institutions are nascent and unstable.

The report is structured as follows: chapter 2 presents a diagnostic of the labor force in Libya using the analysis of the Bureau of Statistics and Census' 2012 Labor Force Survey. To address how Libya can start to address constraints arising from this analysis, Libya's labor market institutions are assessed in chapter 3. Chapter 4 launches a discussion of possible interventions for the Libyan context from the perspective of job seekers by evaluating their preferences and skills. Chapter 5 takes stock of the outlook of jobs in the private sector from employers' perspectives. Finally, based on these findings, chapter 6 presents a policy framework and recommendations for both the demand and supply sides to promote gainful, stable employment. It is hoped that this assessment will serve as a basis for Libya to develop a jobs strategy based on a vision for a vibrant private sector to move forward.

Notes

1. World Bank. 2014. *Libya Economic Monitoring Note, Spring*. Washington, DC: World Bank.
2. International Monetary Fund (IMF). 2013. *Libya, 2013 Article IV Consultation*. IMF Country Report 13/150, Washington, DC.
3. World Bank. 2014. *Libya Economic Monitoring Note*. Washington, DC: World Bank.
4. Statistical information and data in Libya are sparse, making the present analysis challenging. The Bureau of Statistics and Census (BSC) produces household survey data

every 10 years. Since 2007, BSC has conducted approximately five annual or bi-annual labor force surveys (LFSs). However, only data for the 2010 and 2012 LFSs were deemed reliable enough by the authorities to use for analyses. Since 2012, a capacity-building program has been ongoing to improve macro- and microeconomic datasets at the BSC.

5. To absorb current job seekers into the labor market, preliminary estimates suggest that Libya's economy likely would need to grow by an estimated 6.5 percent annually over 5 years, but by 17 percent for 10 years if relying solely on the private sector. These estimates assume that economic growth translates to labor market growth; and that, based on pre-uprising estimates, an estimated 25,000 graduates per year enter the job market. Both assumptions need to be further evaluated.

6. World Bank, *World Development Report 2011: Conflict, Security, and Development* (Washington, DC: World Bank, 2011).

7. World Bank, *World Development Report 2013: Jobs* (Washington, DC: World Bank, 2012).

8. D. A. Robalino, L. Rawlings, and I. Walker, "Building Social Protection and Labor Systems Concepts and Operational Implications," Social Protection and Labor Discussion Paper 1202 (Washington, DC: World Bank, 2012); G. Betcherman, "Labor Market Institutions: A Review of the Literature," Policy Research Working Paper 6276 (Washington, DC: World Bank, 2012).

9. The Libyan Bureau of Statistics and Census (BSC), under the tutelage of the Ministry of Planning, conducts annual labor force surveys. Between 2007 and 2011, 3 surveys were fielded, but data quality issues remain. As a result, these data were not included in this assessment. The 2012 and 2013 LFS (not yet available) were conducted using updated questionnaires and survey guidelines, with a 2014–15 LFS forthcoming. The sampling frame is based on the BSC's 2010 General Demographic Survey and adopts cluster sampling due to high geographic dispersion in Libya. The 2012 LFS sample comprised 9,340 households and following data cleaning, the final dataset for analysis comprises 9,280 households and 50,256 individuals.

CHAPTER 2

Structure of the Libyan Labor Market

Introduction

In 2013 the population in Libya stood at nearly 6.1 million, of which 84 percent lived in urban areas, primarily along the Mediterranean, where most jobs are generally located.[1] Despite the presence of oil, poverty persists in Libya. In 2003 poverty was approximately 11.8 percent, with wide regional variations across governorates ranging from 1.5 percent to 30 percent.[2]

Libyans also are relatively young compared to their neighbors, with 52 percent aged 24 or younger and fewer than 4 percent aged 64 or older. In line with other middle-income countries facing a youth bulge, 30 percent of the Libyan population is under the age of 14 years. This share is comparable to Kuwait (25 percent), Malaysia (27 percent), and Turkey (26 percent); and is younger than Chile (21 percent) and Tunisia (23 percent). Most Libyans are connected to telecommunications through mobile technology with a high penetration rate of 148 mobile subscriptions per 100 persons. However, internet penetration is among the lowest in the world. In 2012, only 1 in 5 people in Libya were connected to the internet, compared to 4 in 10 in Jordan and Tunisia, 7 in 10 in Malaysia, and 8 in 10 in Kuwait. Against this background, a look at the structure of Libya's labor market in the following sections begins to highlight the importance of targeting key population groups as well as those sectors with the greatest job creation potential, discussed later in the report.

Overview of the Labor Force

Youth (ages 15–24 years) represent 10 percent of the labor force, and females comprise 34 percent of the labor force (Table 2.1 and figure 2.1). The female share of the Libyan labor force is comparable to the share in most middle-income countries including Tunisia (27 percent), Turkey (30 percent), and Malaysia (38 percent). On the other hand, in 2012 Libya's female workforce was far larger than those of neighboring Algeria (17 percent), Jordan (18 percent), and Kuwait (24 percent).[3]

Table 2.1 Summary of Key Labor Market Indicators

Indicator	Male	Female	Total
Working age population (000s)	2,026	1,916	3,942
Labor force (000s)	1,236	647	1,882
Labor force participation rate (%)	61.0	34.0	48.0
Employment (000s)	1,039	485	1,524
Employment to population ratio (%)	51.0	25.0	39.0
Unemployment (000s)	196	162	358
Unemployment rate (%)	15.9	25.1	19.0
Under-employed (000s)	390	83	463
Share of underemployment (%)	31.0	13.0	25.0
Youth employed (000s) (15–24 years)	57	38	95
Youth unemployment rate	40.9	67.9	48.7

Source: World Bank staff and Bureau of Statistics and Census (BSC) calculations, Libya Labor Force Survey (LFS) 2012.

Figure 2.1 Libya's Labor Force by Age and Gender
thousands

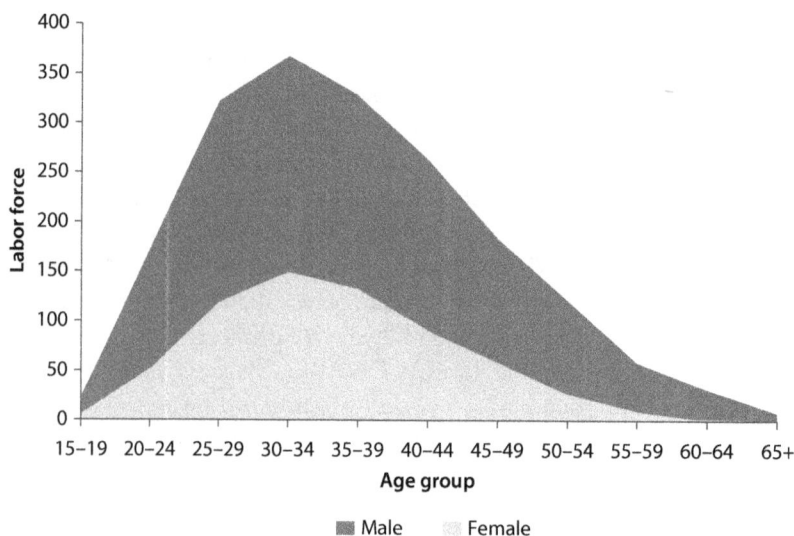

Source: World Bank staff and Bureau of Statistics and Census (BSC) calculations, Libya Labor Force Survey (LFS) 2012.

Regarding educational level, the majority of Libya's labor force is semi-skilled. Approximately half has attained a secondary education or post-secondary training (47 percent) and a small minority have only attained primary education or less (13 percent). Nearly 25 percent of the labor force holds a university degree (figure 2.2 and figure 2.3).

Among Libyan nationals, in 2012 the labor force participation rate (LFPR) (that is, among the working age population) is estimated to have been 47.8 percent, equivalent to nearly 1.9 million Libyan nationals (table 2.1). The active employed

Figure 2.2 Labor Force by Educational Level and Age
percent

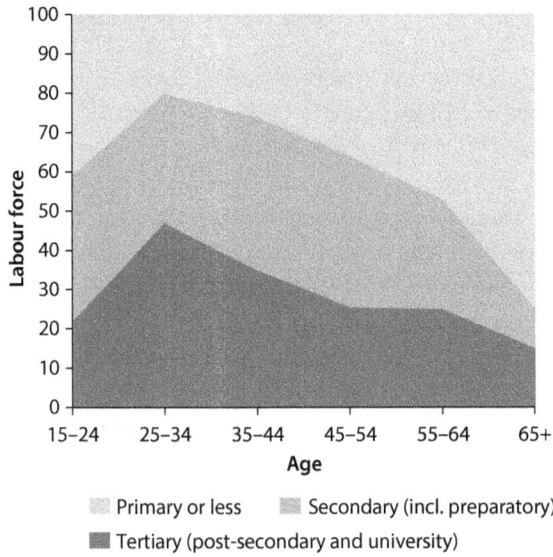

Primary or less   Secondary (incl. preparatory)
Tertiary (post-secondary and university)

Source: World Bank staff and Bureau of Statistics and Census (BSC) calculations, Libya Labor Force Survey (LFS) 2012.

Figure 2.3 Labor Force by Educational Level: International Comparisons
percent

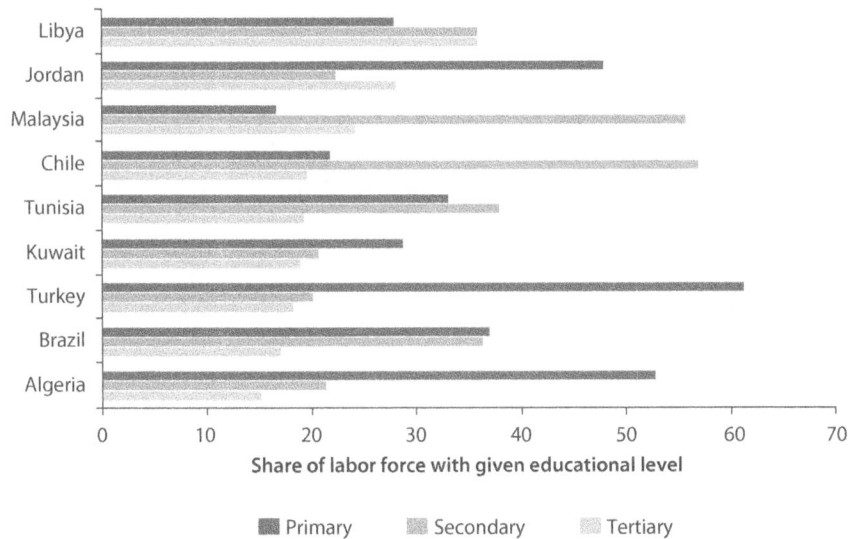

Primary   Secondary   Tertiary

Source: World Bank staff and BSC calculations, Libya LFS 2012, World Development Indicators (WDI) and (International Labour Organization) ILO Key Indicators of the Labour Market (KILM) database 2013, http://www.ilo.org/empelm/what/WCMS_114240/lang--en/index.htm.

population stands at 1.5 million Libyan nationals. The resulting overall employ-
ment-to-population ratio is estimated at 38.7 percent. This share is relatively low
compared to the Middle East and North Africa average of 43 percent and 54.8
percent among other middle-income countries.

In line with other Middle East and North Africa countries,[4] Libya's labor market reveals wide gender disparities in LFPR (figure 2.4). Libya's overall LFPR is
in line with other Middle East and North Africa countries, yet far lower than
other emerging economies such as Malaysia, Peru, and South Africa. Whereas
Libya's LFPR among males is approximately 61 percent, it is nearly half of that
number among females, at 33.8 percent. However, because of ambiguities in the
definition and the structure of employment in Libya, these rates should be interpreted cautiously, as detailed below.

Prior to the 2011 conflict, the foreign labor force comprised an estimated 1.2
million–1.5 million, accounting for approximately 50 percent of the total
pre-conflict labor force of 2.6 million. In 2012, it is estimated that approximately

Figure 2.4   Labor Force Participation Rate (LFPR), 2012
percent

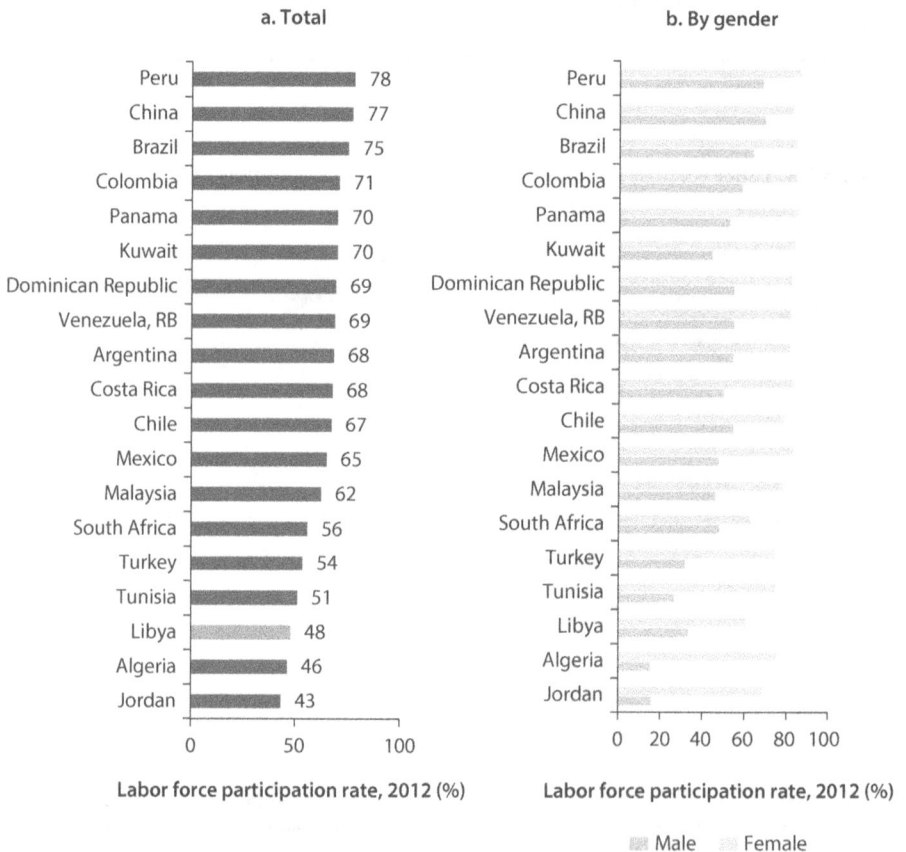

a. Total

Country	LFPR
Peru	78
China	77
Brazil	75
Colombia	71
Panama	70
Kuwait	70
Dominican Republic	69
Venezuela, RB	69
Argentina	68
Costa Rica	68
Chile	67
Mexico	65
Malaysia	62
South Africa	56
Turkey	54
Tunisia	51
Libya	48
Algeria	46
Jordan	43

Labor force participation rate, 2012 (%)

b. By gender

Labor force participation rate, 2012 (%)

■ Male   ■ Female

Source: World Bank staff and BSC calculations, Libya Labor Force Survey (LFS) 2012, World Development
Indicators (WDI)/ILO KILM database.

430,000 foreign workers are employed in the formal sector, and another 800,000 workers are employed informally.[5] Combined, foreign workers comprise approximately 40 percent of the labor force; Libyan nationals account for 60 percent.

Foreign workers are an important source of labor in Libya, as one in three firms is unable to find qualified Libyans for jobs.[6] Challenges to recruitment are especially evident for more highly skilled jobs in the oil and gas sector—jobs that typically are filled by foreign workers. Libya's foreign workers range from highly skilled professionals to lower skilled laborers working in manual jobs. The largest group of foreign workers includes nationals of neighboring Middle East and North Africa countries (Egyptians, Mauritanians, Moroccans, Sudanese, and Tunisians) followed by nationals from African countries (Chadians, Eritreans, Ghanaians, Malians, Nigerians, and Somalis),[7] as well as workers from other countries including Bangladesh, Serbia, and Ukraine.

The uprising in Libya gave rise to militia, who offered attractive benefits for the unemployed. During the conflict, nearly 300,000 Libyan nationals joined such informal organizations in a spectrum of combative roles, most of whom are males. Figure 2.5, which reflects data from the Warriors' Affairs Commission (WAC) survey of 225,000 people involved in the conflict, shows the diversity of occupational backgrounds of those fighters. Notably, a large proportion of those involved in the conflict were unemployed. This fact indicates that formal and informal security organizations may well have provided temporarily employment opportunity for Libyans who previously may not have been successful in the labor

Figure 2.5 Job Seekers Registered with WAC by Pre-Conflict Employment Status, 2012

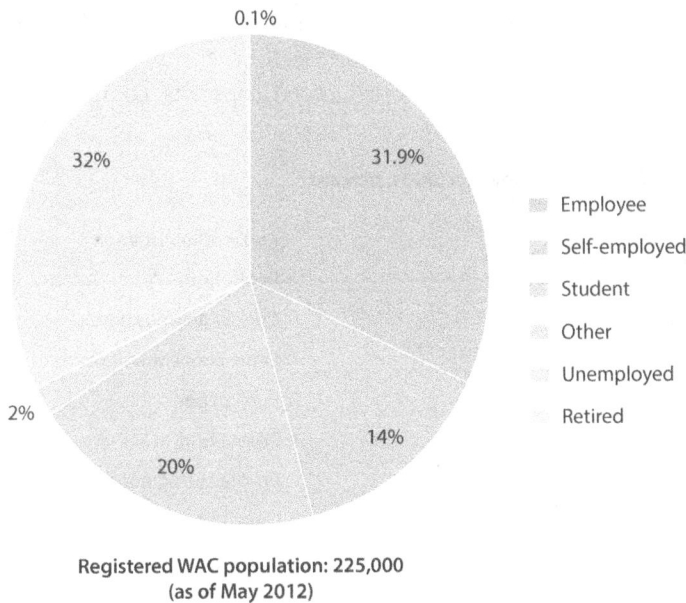

0.1%

32%

31.9%

2%

14%

20%

Employee

Self-employed

Student

Other

Unemployed

Retired

Registered WAC population: 225,000
(as of May 2012)

Source: Warriors Affairs Commission communication, May 2012.

market due to a lack of skills and motivation. Of the 225,000 jobseekers registered at WAC in early 2012, approximately 32 percent had classified themselves as unemployed and 14 percent as self-employed.

Where Are the Jobs?

The vast majority of the employed in Libya work in the public sector (84 percent in 2012), which is considered high even by regional standards (figure 2.6). The rate is even higher for females. Ninety-seven percent of all working women are employed in the public sector compared to 79 percent of working males (figure 2.7). These figures are not surprising given the structure of the Libyan economy, which is dominated by state-owned enterprises (SOEs) and the oil sector, which employs a relatively small proportion of the labor force. In addition, the self-employment rate in Libya, estimated at 6.8 percent, is far lower than that observed in neighboring Maghreb countries (26.1 percent).

Compared to the Middle East and North Africa average and to other middle-income countries, employment in industry and agriculture is considerably lower in Libya (figure 2.8 and figure 2.9). These two sectors account for only 9 percent and 1 percent of the labor force, respectively. In 1986 industry accounted for 30 percent of employment; in 2012 industry accounted for only 9 percent. Over the same period, agriculture plummeted from 20 percent of employment to 1 percent. In stark contrast, employment in services (largely in the public sector) has expanded to over 70 percent of today's active labor force.

Contracts and Social Insurance Coverage

The majority of employed Libyans tend to have open-ended contracts. This pattern is driven largely by the dominance of the public sector as the main employer. Ninety-four percent of civil servants have open-ended contracts, compared to

Figure 2.6   Libya's Labor Force by Occupation (000s, percent)

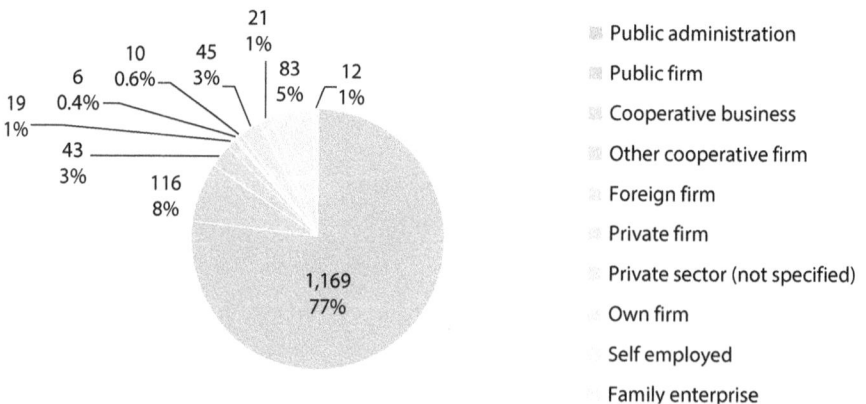

Legend:
- Public administration
- Public firm
- Cooperative business
- Other cooperative firm
- Foreign firm
- Private firm
- Private sector (not specified)
- Own firm
- Self employed
- Family enterprise

Source: World Bank staff and Bureau of Statistics and Census (BSC) calculations, Libya Labor Force Survey (LFS) 2012.

Figure 2.7 Libya's Occupational Distribution by Gender
percent

a. Males

Private - self - employed 10.5

Private - wage 11

Public sector (total) 78.5

b. Females

Private - wage 2.5

Private - self - employed 1

Public sector (total) 96.5

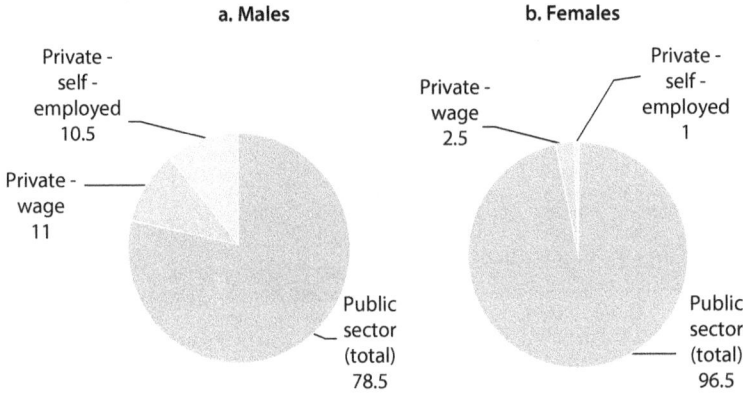

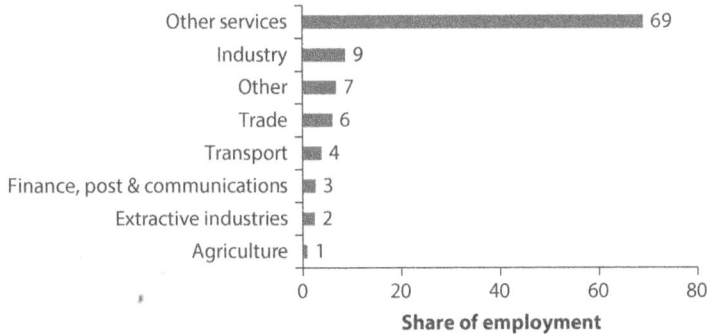

Source: World Bank staff and Bureau of Statistics and Census (BSC) calculations, Libya Labor Force Survey (LFS) 2012.

Figure 2.8 Distribution of Employment by Economic Sector
percent

Sector	Share of employment
Other services	69
Industry	9
Other	7
Trade	6
Transport	4
Finance, post & communications	3
Extractive industries	2
Agriculture	1

Source: World Bank staff and Bureau of Statistics and Census (BSC) calculations, Libya Labor Force Survey (LFS) 2012.

81 percent of the labor force in the private sector (figure 2.10). Among the latter, 89 percent of those who are 45 years or older report having open-ended contracts. The estimate drops to 67 percent among youth. These rates among youth could be driven by various forms of self-employment and/or short-term training contracts mandated under Libyan law. The latter potentially create incentives to expand "training" as a substitute for formal employment or longer term contracts. According to qualitative survey work conducted for this report, some civil servants reported also working in the private sector, either as salaried workers without contracts or as self-employed.

Overall, 90 percent of the Libyan workforce reports being enrolled in some form of social security, but the difference between the public and private sectors

Figure 2.9 Distribution of Employment in Key Sectors: International Comparisons, 2012
percent

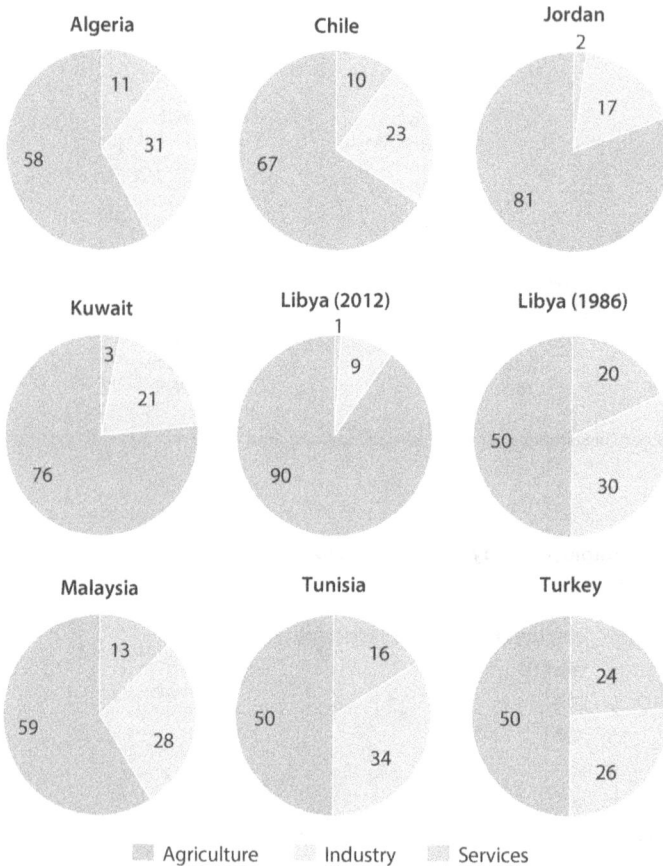

Algeria: 58, 11, 31

Chile: 67, 10, 23

Jordan: 2, 17, 81

Kuwait: 76, 3, 21

Libya (2012): 90, 1, 9

Libya (1986): 50, 20, 30

Malaysia: 59, 13, 28

Tunisia: 50, 16, 34

Turkey: 50, 24, 26

■ Agriculture   ■ Industry   ■ Services

Source: World Bank staff calculations, Libya Labor Force Survey (LFS) 2012, World Development Indicators (WDI) and ILO KILM database.

is striking (figure 2.12). To draw international comparisons, the precise definition of social security coverage in the Libyan context will need further exploration. While 98 percent of public sector workers are covered, the rate in the private sector is nearly half this rate at only 46 percent. Tax wedge data[8] suggest that Libya is generally at the lower end of the spectrum (figure 2.11). Additional data are needed to better evaluate the tax wedge.

Age groups with the lowest levels of open-ended contracts tend to report the lowest rates of social security coverage (figure 2.12). At 37–39 percent, 15–34-year-olds report the lowest rates of coverage. The rate increases gradually to 66 percent among 55–64-year-olds. The rate drops again to 41 percent among 65-year-olds and older, suggesting that social insurance among workers retired from the "private" sector is weak. Detailed data on informality were not available at the time of writing, but this data suggest that overall, approximately 5 percent

Figure 2.10 Type of Employment Contract by Sector and Age

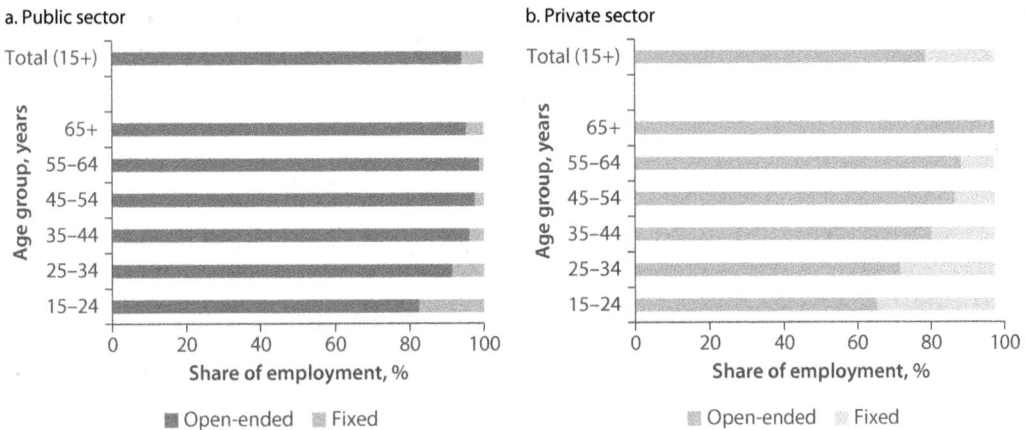

a. Public sector

b. Private sector

Source: World Bank staff calculations, Libya Labor Force Survey (LFS) 2012.

Figure 2.11 Tax Wedge: International Comparisons

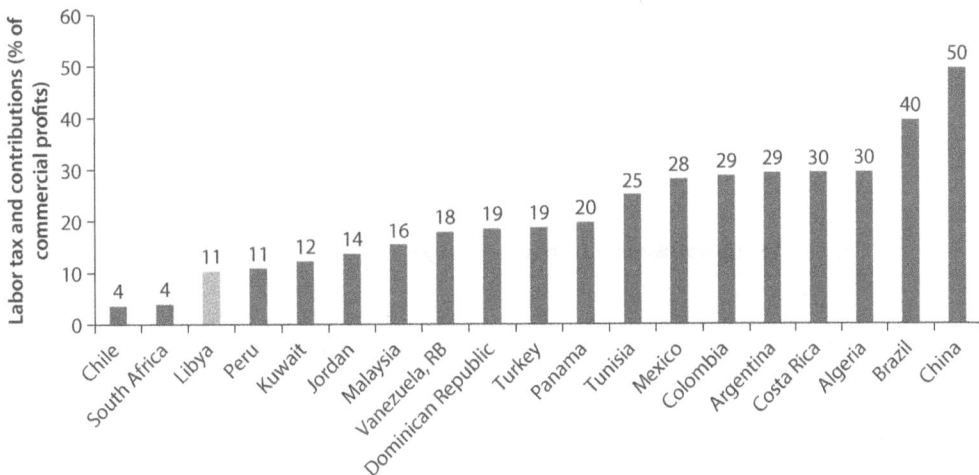

Source: World Bank staff calculations, Libya Labor Force Survey (LFS) 2012, World Development Indicators (WDI) and ILO KILM database.

of those working today in Libya are informal (that is, do not contribute to social security coverage). This rate is largely accounted for by the sizable share of private sector employment that is considered informal.

Wages and Earnings

The wage distribution shows that the average wage is approximately 791 LYD per month, or the equivalent of US$7,474 per year, which is buttressed by substantive state subsidies on fuel, food, and benefits (figure 2.13 and figure 2.14). Average wages range from 597 LYD among local private firms to 1,195 LYD among foreign firms (or US$5,641–11,291 per year). In contrast, civil servants

Figure 2.12 Social Security Coverage by Sector and Age

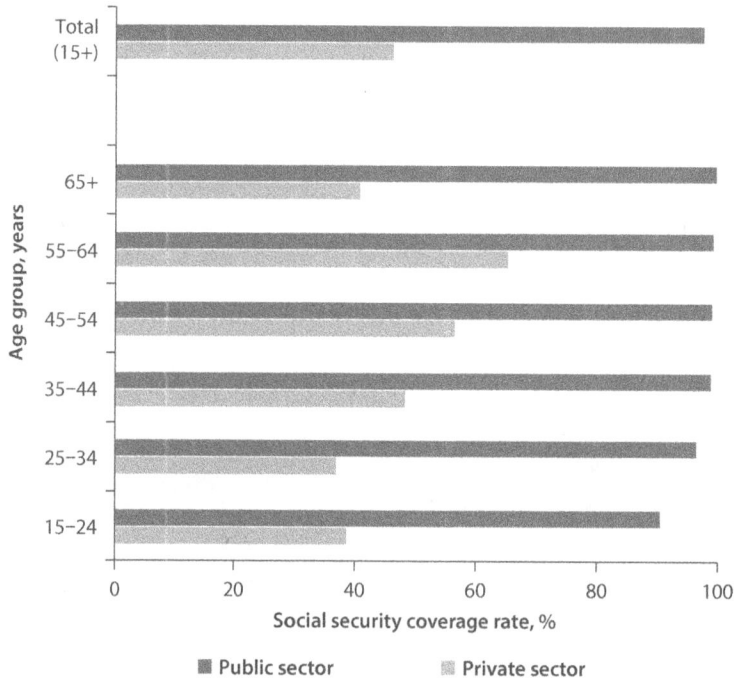

Source: World Bank staff calculations, Libya Labor Force Survey (LFS) 2012.

Figure 2.13 Overall Wage Distribution in Libya

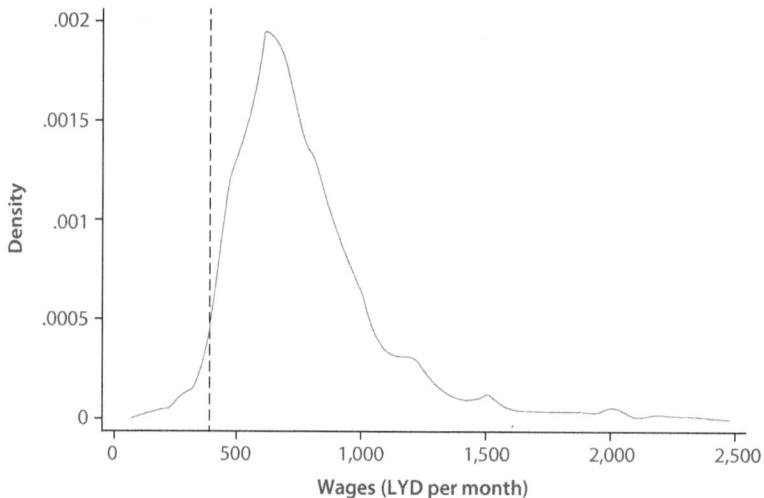

Source: World Bank staff calculations, Libya Labor Force Survey (LFS) 2012.

working in the Libyan public administration tend to earn 755 LYD per month (US$7,134 per year), and civil servants in SOEs earn on average 934 LYD per month (US$8,825 per year), or 24 percent higher.

Due to data limitations, wage comparisons between the private and public sectors are difficult to draw with a high degree of confidence. In comparison to the public sector and foreign firms, local private firms tend to offer the lowest wages (figure 2.15).

Estimating the economic returns to education requires more precise data, but the trends suggest that, first, university-level education yields additional modest returns relative to secondary education, particularly in the private sector. Overall, university graduates tend to earn 12 percent more than secondary graduates,

Figure 2.14 Wage Distribution by Sector in Libya

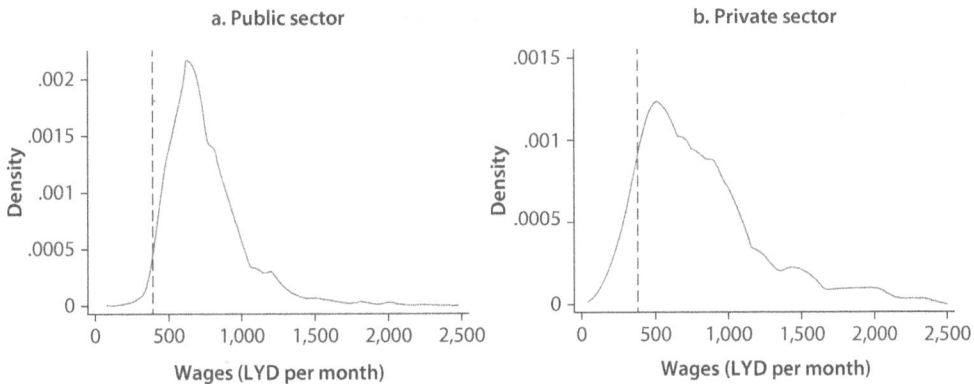

a. Public sector

b. Private sector

Source: World Bank staff calculations, Libya Labor Force Survey (LFS) 2012.

Figure 2.15 Average Wages per Capita by Occupational Category and Relative Share

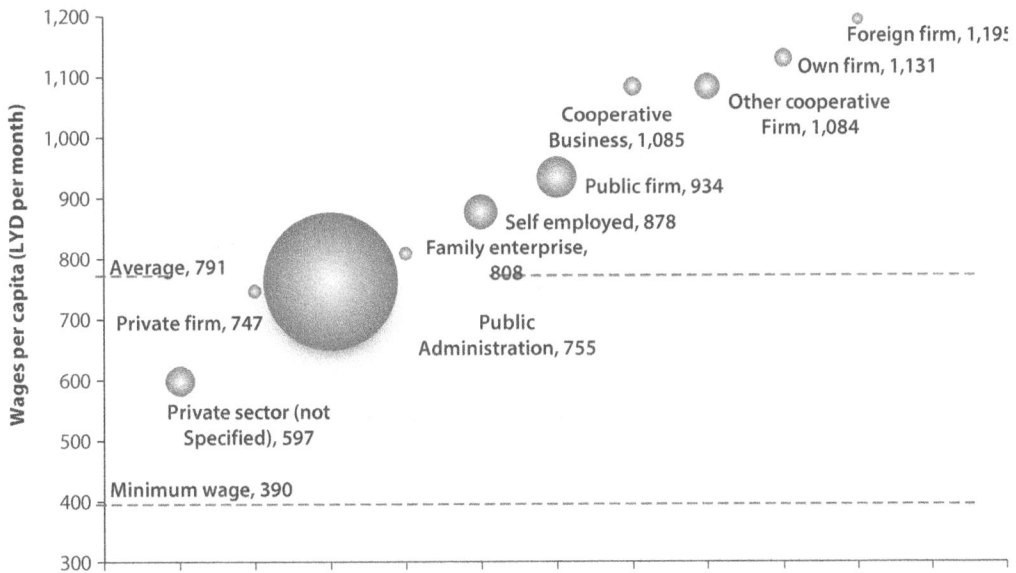

Source: World Bank staff calculations, Libya Labor Force Survey (LFS) 2012.

which breaks out as 21 percent more in the private sector and 11 percent more in the public sector (figure 2.16). At all levels of education, income levels are 17 percent higher on average in the private sector than in the public sector, particularly among university graduates (figure 2.17). However, as mentioned, these trends suggest that the "public" and "private" sectors in Libya are heterogeneous and not always clearly demarcated.

Wages among females with a secondary education tend to be three times higher in the public sector than in the private sector. These data should be

Figure 2.16 Tertiary versus Secondary Education Wage Premium by Gender and Sector

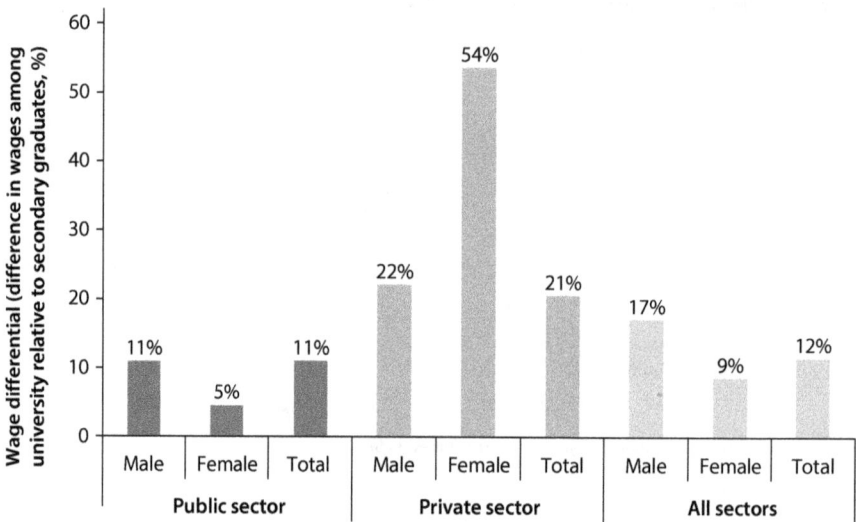

Source: World Bank staff calculations, Libya Labor Force Survey (LFS) 2012.

Figure 2.17 Wage Differentials between Private and Public Sectors by Educational Level

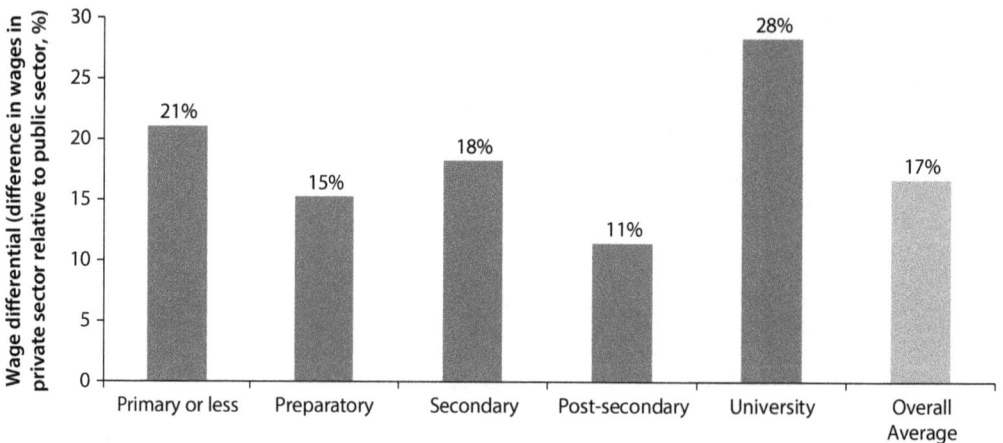

Source: World Bank staff calculations, Libya Labor Force Survey (LFS) 2012.

considered cautiously since, given the small sample size in the private sector, educational returns by gender are difficult to evaluate. Female university gradu- ates tend to earn 18 percent less than their male public sector counterparts and 11 percent less in the private sector. Females who finished secondary school earn 30 percent less than their male counterparts in the private sector, and 10 percent less than males in the public sector. Within the public sector, although qualitative interviews with the public administration suggest that wages are fixed by grade regardless of gender, these data suggest that hiring and place- ment practices may reflect wage differentials. For example, women may be more likely to be found in lower-grade positions than higher-grade positions. These data also suggest that the returns to education are borne mainly by female university graduates in the private sector than any other group. However, more data are needed to more precisely evaluate these trends.

Overall, women tend to earn 12 percent less than men in Libya—an outcome driven largely by a 7 percent differential in public administration and 20 percent in SOEs. Estimated wage differentials by gender in the public sector are more reliable than those in the private sector due to limited data in the latter. Trends suggest that males earn more than women among local private firms but that women earn somewhat more than men among the self-employed and foreign firms. These differences could be driven by self-selection bias. In other words, the few women who opt out of the public sector may possess particular skills, com- petencies, or networks that distinguish them from their male counterparts, many more of whom are found in the private sector.

As observed in other countries, Libyan university graduates tend to earn more than their nongraduate counterparts. Additional data are needed to ascertain these returns in more detail, particularly given that Libya has one of the highest rates of unemployment relative to tertiary enrollment. This finding suggests that the quality of, hence the returns to, education may be sub-par.

Underemployment also is pervasive in Libya, particularly among males and youth. Eighty-two percent of employed individuals report working an average of 40–48 hours per week. Thirty percent of the active labor force report being underemployed. Of those who want more hours, 37 percent are male and 17 percent are females (figure 2.18). Underemployment also is somewhat higher in the public sector, particularly among 45–54-year-olds, who also tend to have the highest rate of open-ended contracts, second only to 55–64-year-olds.

Who and Where Are the Unemployed?

Following the 2011 uprising, unemployment has increased steadily in Libya, reaching 19.0 percent, or 358,300 individuals, in 2012, up from an estimated 13.5 percent in 2010. Libya's unemployment rate is one of the highest among middle-income countries. Lower than that of South Africa (25 percent), unem- ployment in Libya is comparable to that of Tunisia (18 percent) but double the rate in Turkey (9 percent) (figure 2.19).

Figure 2.18   Distribution of Age-Specific Underemployment Rates by Gender and Sector

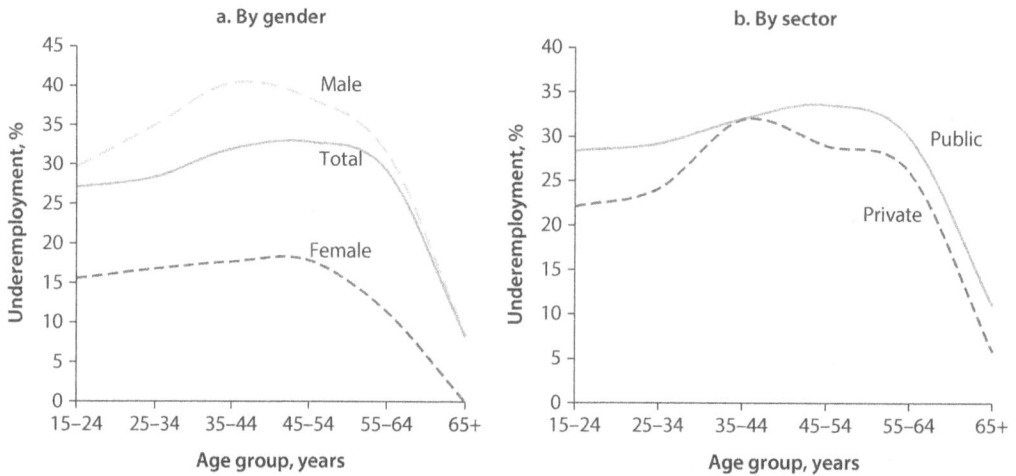

Source: World Bank staff calculations, Libya Labor Force Survey (LFS) 2012.
Note: Calculations are based on % of respondents who "want more working hours."

As seen in most of the Middle East and North Africa region, female unemployment is higher than that of males—25 percent compared to 16 percent in 2012 (figure 2.20). Similar to other Middle East and North Africa countries, these gender dynamics in the Libyan labor market likely are the result of lower labor mobility among females; preference for public sector jobs, which come with generous nonwage benefits such as those for maternity; and other factors related to lagging private sector job growth.

Overall, Libya's unemployment also varies widely by region, particularly in the west. Unemployment generally is higher in the western half of the country, including Tripoli and Misratah, compared to Benghazi (figure 2.21). Additional data are needed to evaluate underlying factors that may contribute to regional variations in unemployment.

Ministry of Labor and Manpower (MOL) data suggest that there were 400,000 registered job seekers in 2013, including employed and unemployed individuals. Of this estimate, 290,000 were unemployed. It is important to note that the figures for overall labor force participation, employment, and unemployment are not necessarily the same as the figures of those jobseekers who register looking for unemployment support. Registration represents the *demand* for services, not necessarily the *extent* of unemployment per se. The demand may exceed, be equal to, or be less than the actual level of unemployment in a given country, depending on incentives for seeking services and other factors that may induce both employed and unemployed to seek government support.

Not controlling for other factors, while no significant differences in unemployment rates are seen by education level among males, unemployment is higher

Figure 2.19 Unemployment Rate, Overall and by Gender: International Comparisons

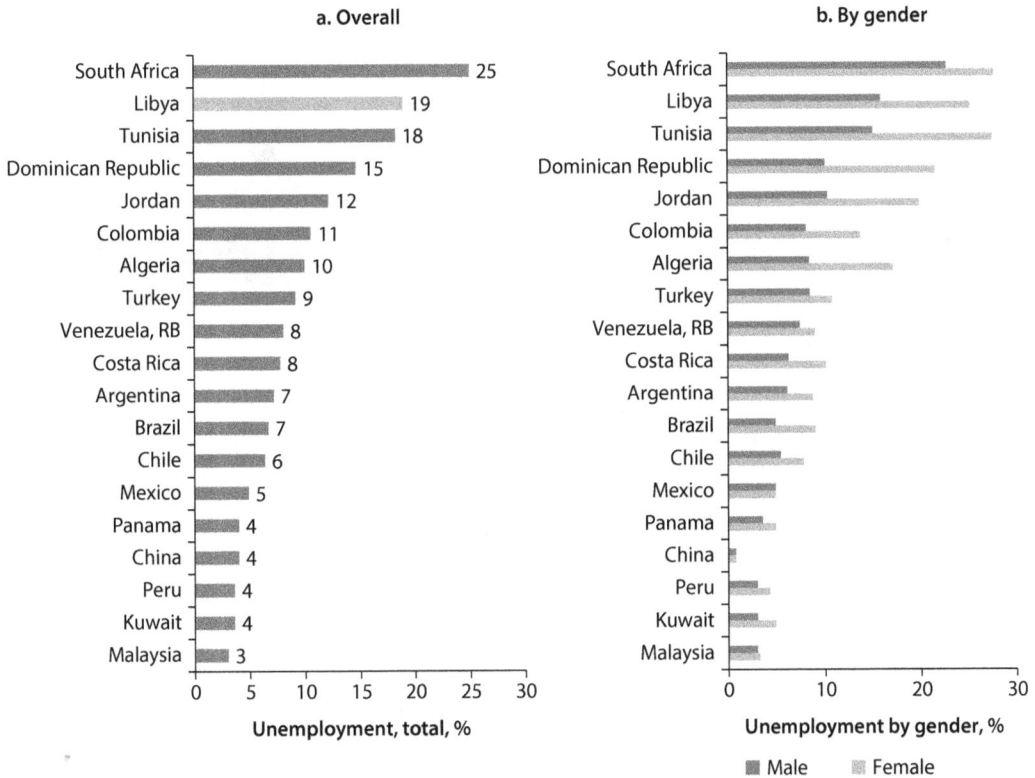

percent

a. Overall

b. By gender

	Unemployment, total, %
South Africa	25
Libya	19
Tunisia	18
Dominican Republic	15
Jordan	12
Colombia	11
Algeria	10
Turkey	9
Venezuela, RB	8
Costa Rica	8
Argentina	7
Brazil	7
Chile	6
Mexico	5
Panama	4
China	4
Peru	4
Kuwait	4
Malaysia	3

b. By gender — Unemployment by gender, %

South Africa, Libya, Tunisia, Dominican Republic, Jordan, Colombia, Algeria, Turkey, Venezuela, RB, Costa Rica, Argentina, Brazil, Chile, Mexico, Panama, China, Peru, Kuwait, Malaysia

■ Male   ▨ Female

Source: World Bank staff and Bureau of Statistics and Census (BSC) calculations, Libya Labor Force Survey (LFS) 2012, World Development Indicators (WDI) and ILO KILM database 2013.

Figure 2.20 Unemployment Rate by Age and Gender

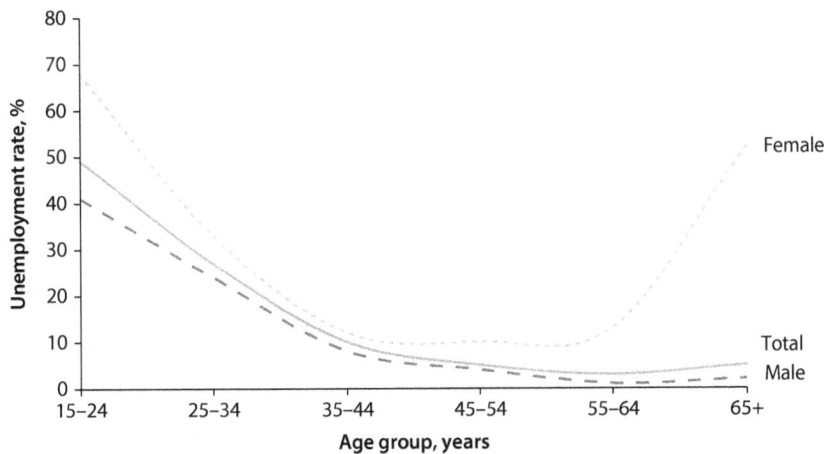

Female

Total

Male

Age group, years: 15–24, 25–34, 35–44, 45–54, 55–64, 65+

Source: World Bank staff and Bureau of Statistics and Census (BSC) calculations, Libya Labor Force Survey (LFS) 2012.

Labor Market Dynamics in Libya • http://dx.doi.org/10.1596/978-1-4648-0566-0

Map 2.1 Unemployment Rate in Libya by Governorate
percent

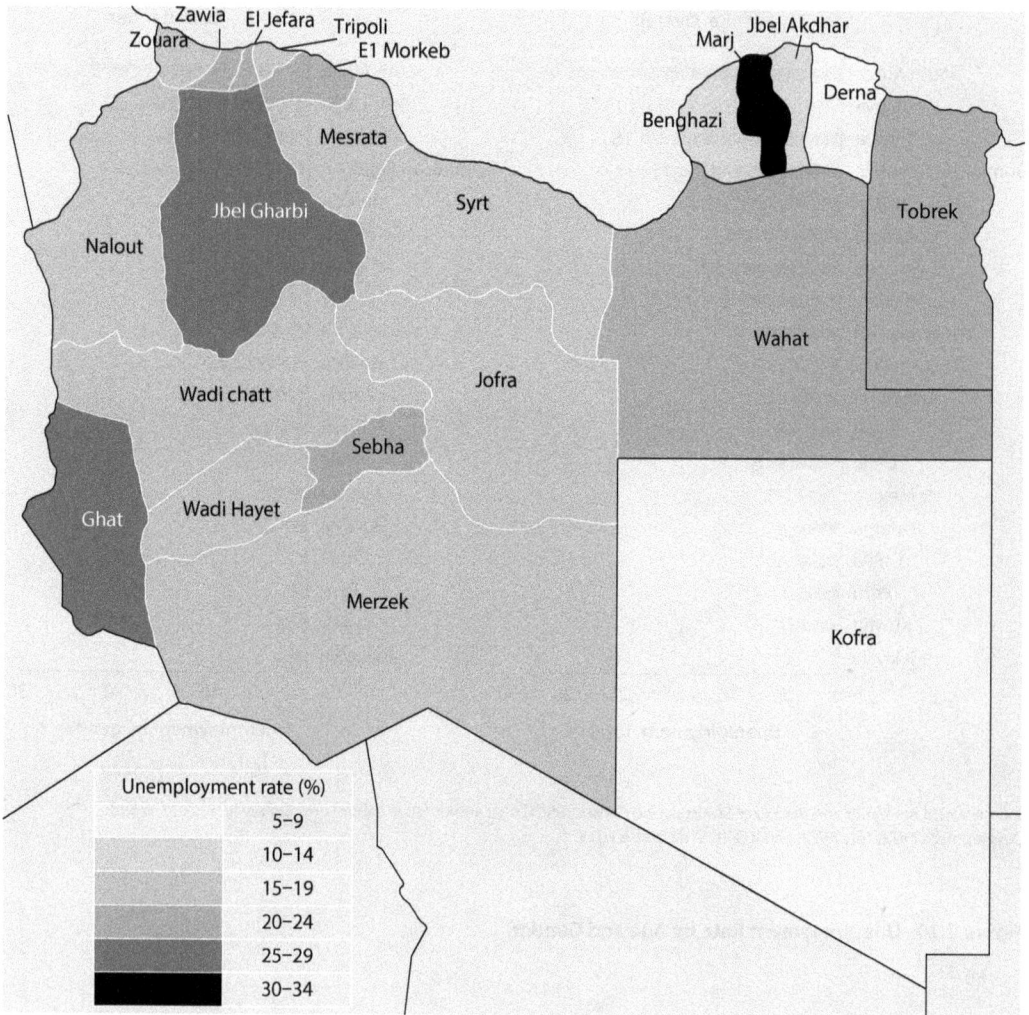

Source: World Bank staff and Bureau of Statistics and Census (BSC) calculations, Libya Labor Force Survey (LFS) 2012.

among lower educational levels among females (primary or less) (figure 2.21). At the same time, at 25 percent, unemployment among females with a university education is still high compared to other middle-income countries. These patterns may reflect either a lack of jobs for unskilled Libyan females or a lower willingness of Libyan females, compared to Libyan males, to accept low-skilled jobs.

Overall, Libya also has a particularly high rate of unemployment coupled with a high tertiary enrollment rate—seemingly a paradox (figure 2.22). However, there is a notable gradual increase in female tertiary education relative to males over time, which may be indicative of broader social factors (figure 2.23).

Figure 2.21 Unemployment Rate in Libya by Gender and Educational Level

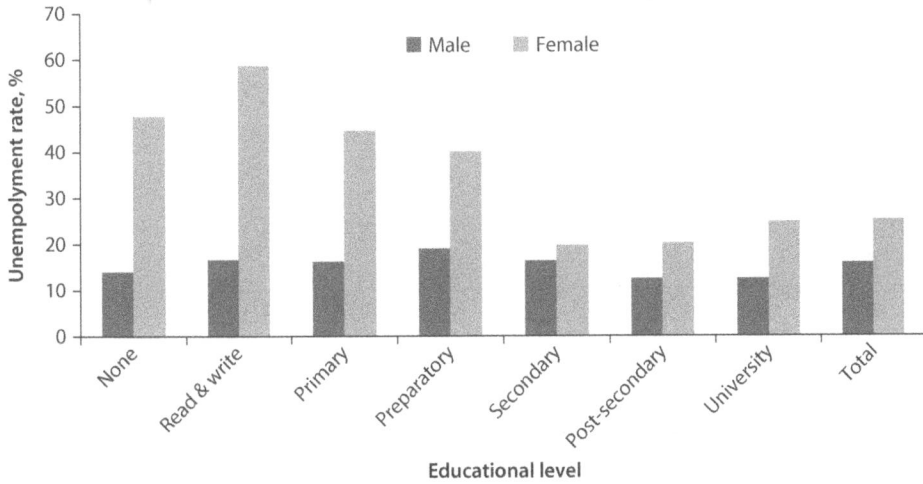

Source: World Bank staff and Bureau of Statistics and Census (BSC) calculations, Libya Labor Force Survey (LFS) 2012.

Figure 2.22 Unemployment Rates by Tertiary Enrollment: International Comparisons

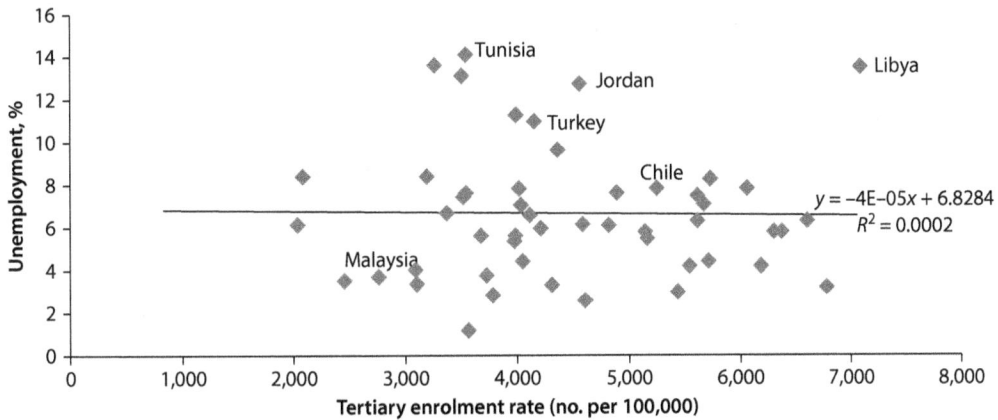

$$y = -4\text{E}{-}05x + 6.8284$$
$$R^2 = 0.0002$$

Source: World Bank staff and Bureau of Statistics and Census (BSC) calculations, Libya Labor Force Survey 2012, World Development Indicators, World Bank, and UNESCO Education Statistics 2013.
Note: The most recent education data shown for Libya (2003).

Youth unemployment in Libya, estimated at 48 percent, is particularly high compared to other Middle East and North Africa and middle-income countries (figure 2.24). Higher unemployment persists among the 25–34 age group compared to the national average of 19 percent. After age 35, unemployment drops 67 percent from 27.3 percent to 9.5 percent for those aged 35–44, then to only 5.2 percent for ages 45–54. These unemployment patterns may indicate a slow

Figure 2.23   Libya's Tertiary Enrollment over Time: Total and by Gender, 1992–2003

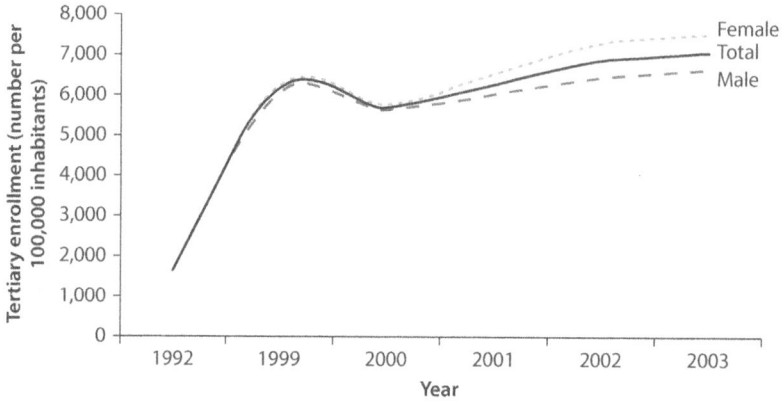

Source: World Development Indicators, World Bank, and United Nations Educational, Scientific, and Cultural Organization (UNESCO) Education Statistics 2013.

Figure 2.24   Youth Unemployment Rate (a) Overall and (b) by Gender
percent

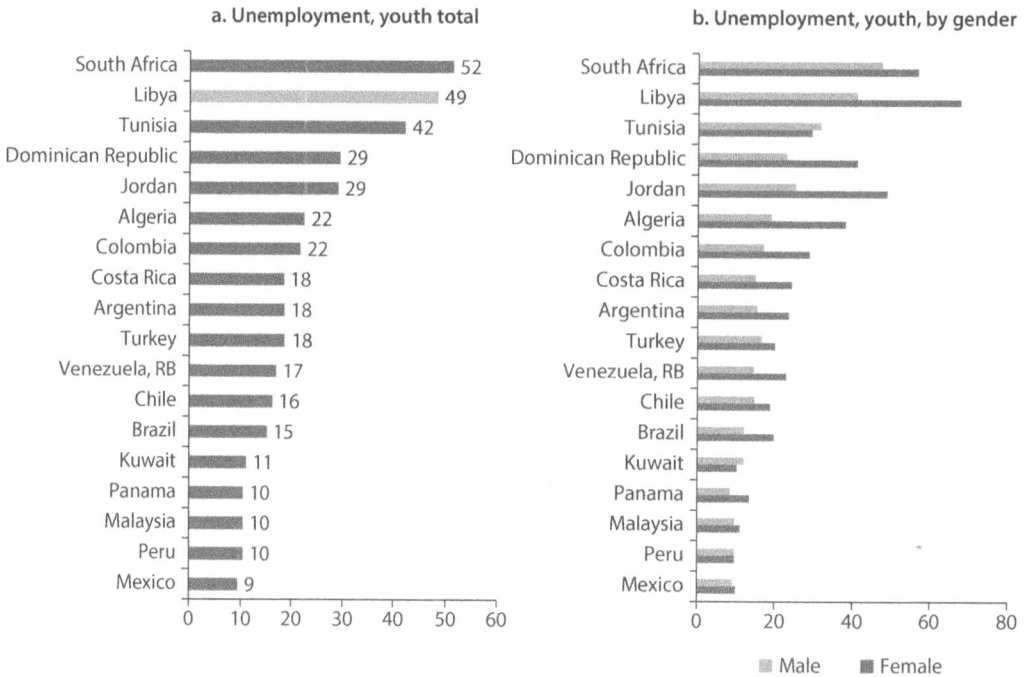

Source: World Bank staff and Bureau of Statistics and Census (BSC) calculations, Libya Labor Force Survey (LFS) 2012, World Development Indicators (WDI) and ILO KILM database 2013.

and inefficient transition from school to work for youth and long queues for public sector jobs. In addition, a substantial number of youth, estimated at 207,000 (of which 112,000 are female), are not enrolled in education or training, further increasing the likelihood of adverse social costs associated with frustration and economic uncertainty among youth.

Conclusions

After the flight of many foreign laborers during the uprising, based on 2012 data, Libya's labor force stands at an estimated 1.9 million, of whom only 34 percent are women. Prior to the uprising, Libya's labor force comprised nearly 2.6 million workers, nearly 50 percent of whom were foreign. Libya's active labor force now comprises 1.5 million workers. The vast majority (84 percent) of the employed in Libya are found in the public sector—a high number even by regional standards—and higher still for women (93 percent). As a corollary, employment in industry (largely the oil sector) and agriculture accounts for only 10 percent of the labor force—20 percent of the level seen nearly 30 years ago. Given the dominance of the public sector as the main employer, job security is high, particularly for 45-year-olds and above, who tend to have open-ended contracts. Moreover, nearly all public sector workers are covered by some form of social insurance. In contrast, only 46 percent of private sector workers are enrolled—a striking difference. Wages in Libya are buttressed by substantive state subsidies on fuel, food, and benefits.

Libya has one of the highest unemployment rates in the world relative to its rate of tertiary enrollment, highlighting both the lack of labor demand and a skills mismatch. Unemployment increased from 13.5 percent in 2010 to 19.0 percent in 2012. In 2012 youth unemployment was estimated at 48 percent and female unemployment at 25 percent. Given the inflated public sector and the limited options in the private sector, these patterns likely reflect a lack of jobs for both skilled and unskilled Libyans, job queuing for public sector jobs, inefficient school-to-work transitions, and a low willingness for Libyans to accept certain positions. The 2010 Investment Climate Assessment (ICA) showed that 30 percent of firms reported difficulties in recruiting Libyan nationals. For Libyans to move ahead, improving job preparedness and skills matching to the needs of an emerging private sector will prove vital.

Notes

1. Libyan Population Survey, Bureau of Census and Statistics, 2012.
2. World Bank, *Libya: A Public Expenditure Review*, 3 vols. (Washington, DC: World Bank, 2009). See detailed poverty data in vol. 3, *Appendixes and Statistical Appendix*.
3. World Bank, *World Development Indicators (WDI)* (Washington, DC: World Bank, 2013).
4. World Bank, *Free to Prosper: Jobs in the Middle East and North Africa* (Washington, DC: World Bank, 2012).
5. Estimates provided by Bureau of Statistics and Census and Ministry of Labor, Libya.
6. World Bank, *Libya Investment Climate Assessment* (Washington, DC: World Bank, 2011), 61.
7. See, for example, International Centre for Migration Policy Development (ICMPD), 2010, "A Comprehensive Survey of Migration Flows and Institutional Capabilities in Libya," Vienna, 28–36.
8. "Tax wedge" refers to labor tax and contributions measured as the amount of taxes and mandatory contributions on labor paid by businesses (WDI).

CHAPTER 3

Building Labor Market Institutions and Policies

Introduction

With a new constitution under preparation beginning in 2013, Libya has a critical need to improve how its labor market institutions function. Making these improvements entails a dual track: (a) building the capacity of Libyan public institutions and (b) strengthening the role of the private sector. Ongoing efforts to institute modern public financial management (PFM) systems and strengthen policy-making capacity had begun in 2012.[1] Developing a mature, well-functioning labor market will entail enhancing labor market (a) policies, (b) programs, (c) partnerships, and (d) information.

The limited capacity of public institutions and lack of reliable data are obstacles to design and implement programs that can address immediate needs as well as to develop strategies and policies for the medium and long terms. Partnerships among the Government of Libya (GOL) and private and civil stakeholders at the local, regional, and global levels will be strategically important to harness the willingness and capacity of partners to help overcome these challenges. This chapter will provide an assessment of labor market institutions in Libya, helping to understand the relationships, roles, and political economy of the institutional landscape.

Emerging Supply-Side Actors

Libya's labor market landscape is in the midst of transition (figure 3.1). The labor force is served primarily by the Ministry of Labor and Manpower (MOL). In addition, a dedicated commission has been created to advocate for and serve ex-combatants: the Warriors Affairs Commission (WAC), which reports to the Prime Ministry. The Ministry of Social Affairs manages the national Social Security Fund, which covers workers in the public and private sectors as well as the self-employed. Benefits include old age, maternity, disability and support for loss of employment, and death. Health services are covered primarily by the state

Figure 3.1 Main Labor Market Actors and Institutions in Libya, 2014

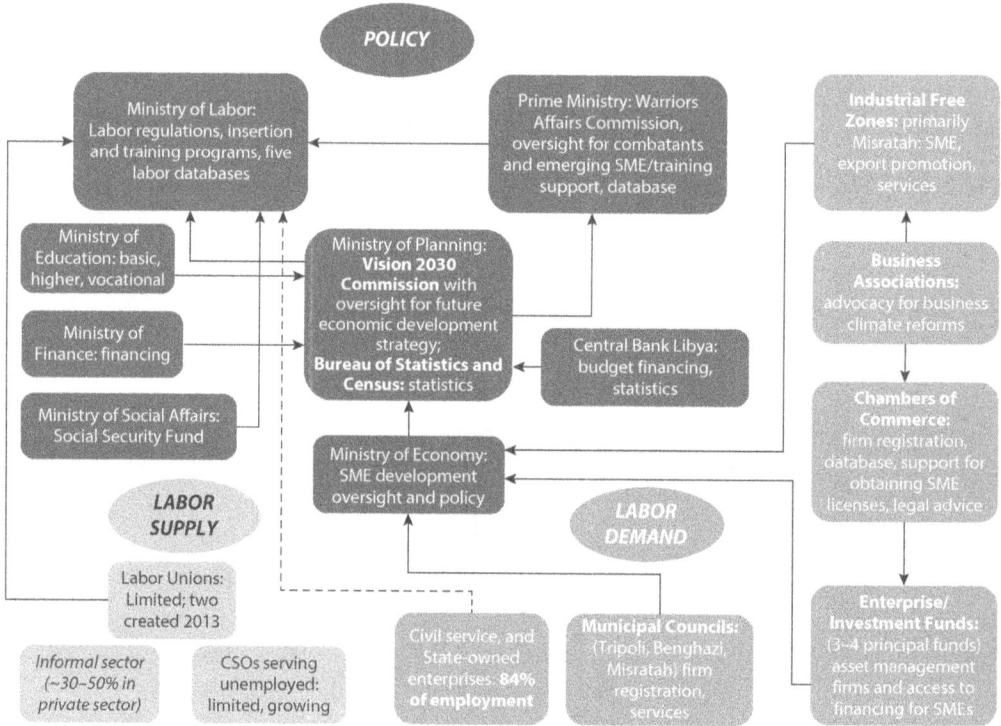

Source: World Bank staff.
Note: SME = small and medium enterprise.

budget. An in-depth evaluation of social security is outside the scope of this assessment, but previous analysis suggests that the social protection system in Libya is unsustainable.[2] In addition, following the uprising, Libya's first labor unions (approximately two) have arisen, as well as a limited number of associations dedicated to training or employment support. Given the paucity of information on the latter, MOL remains the primary state liaison with some of the WAC programs.

MOL is responsible for labor regulations, training, and civil service oversight and, in principle, serves as the primary point of contact for job seekers. MOL facilitates job placement by managing local employment bureaus, which primarily serve to register job seekers into a national, centrally managed database. Six employment bureaus exist in Tripoli with an estimated total of 30 across Libya. More information is needed to assess how registration is conducted and the proportion of Libya's unemployed who register at job service offices. As noted above, MOL oversees civil service staffing as well as training and capacity building programs, which are run largely through contracts with public and private sector providers. Regarding its relationship with the private sector, the ministry has established a limited dialogue, mainly with large foreign firms and particularly for highly skilled labor, such as engineers. Most private Libyan firms recruit their own workers.

The comprehensiveness and accuracy of MOL labor databases are not known. Furthermore, monitoring and evaluation (M&E) are not routinely conducted, making it difficult to improve the efficiency of transitions to work.[3] MOL maintains five employment databases, created in 2007. They are the jobseekers' database, civil service database, surplus staffing database, student database, and loans database to list people who received micro and small business loans. There are no databases for formal or informal foreign workers. The civil service database comprised registration for approximately 1 million civil servants in 2013. The database is used to facilitate job placement in public sector jobs and occasionally for referrals to highly skilled jobs in the private sector.

Active labor market programs in Libya are relatively nascent. For the near term, the plans are to increase MOL's capacity for training, skills development, and job placement programs. Since 2012, given the need to rapidly find solutions for the unemployed and ex-combatants, MOL has managed two main training programs under an emergency framework. The first program targets university graduates interested in information technology and English language skills (spanning three to four months). The second program targets a range of vocational training (six to eight months). These programs are financed by the MOL through direct-to-provider contracts with international and local providers. However, the nature and quality of these providers is unknown to Bank staff. Precise registration, matching, and financing arrangements also are unclear. In 2012 the initial target number of beneficiaries was estimated at 25,000 over five years.

The WAC is recognized as the key body interacting with combatants, established in 2012 as part of the Prime Ministry, although limited coordination also exists with MOL programs. WAC's remit is to coordinate and support disarmament, demobilization, and reintegration (DDR) and economic opportunities for reintegrating ex-combatants into the job market. Since inception, WAC has established dialogue with other Libyan institutions such as the Ministries of Labor, Interior, and Defense and international and bilateral organizations that work on DDR and labor programs. Activities falling under WAC include: (a) registration of ex-combatants seeking reintegration into the WAC database through one of 29 WAC centers nationwide; (b) jobseeker assessments, in which interviews are conducted to assess background, needs and employment aspirations; (c) training, including training entrepreneurship trainers as well as vocational skills development; and (d) small and medium enterprise (SME) grants managed through business incubators throughout Libya. Given the limited M&E systems in place, more information is needed on the progress, nature, coverage, quality, and coordination of these programs with MOL.

Diverse Demand-side Actors

Following the uprising, a range of private-sector-promoting boards and agencies have arisen in Tripoli, Misratah, and Benghazi. They operate nearly independently of one another. The main demand-side actor in Libya is the Ministry of

Economy (MOE), whose main involvement is the National Program for Small and Medium Enterprise (SME) Development. One focus of this program is to facilitate SMEs' access to loans by simplifying the guarantee requirements and interest rates. The MOE also has activities at the city-council level.

The Economic Development Board (EDB), affiliated with the Ministry of Planning (MOP), recently was established to advise MOL and MOE on strategies to boost employment in both public and private sectors. In coordination with WAC, EDB has plans to introduce 20,000 ex-combatants into the labor market.

The Ministry of Planning (MOP) is central to the short- and longer-term development of labor demand in Libya, particularly with the creation of its Vision 2030 Commission. MOP has been involved in developing the new National Development Plan (likely to supersede the old 2008–12 plan). The new plan incorporates the Ministry of Economy's National Program for SME Development, the Ministry of Infrastructure's plans for large public works, and possibly other ministries' future plans. Before the uprising, large public works such as airport construction, the human-made river, and housing developments were large contributors to employment—although not necessarily of Libyans.

The Economic and Social Development Fund (ESDF), or *Al Inma*, is a type of asset management firm. ESDF is the single most important source of private-sector employment in Libya in terms of the combined size of the labor force employed through the firms it represents. The cluster of firms overseen by the ESDF employs an estimated 175,000 Libyans. The ESDF largely defines the direction and pace of Libya's sectoral developments and the extent of any private sector involvement within the sectors, such as selling ESDF banking equity to Qatar National Bank.

Regarding business and trade unions and councils, local city councils, chambers of commerce, and business associations exist in Libya, although with little coordination. At the local level, Tripoli City Council's Economics Department, the local representation of the Ministry of Economy, appears to be one of the strongest actors. The council's agency manages a database of 37,200 firms and conducts reviews to monitor the types, numbers, and needs of these firms.

The mandate of the local chambers of commerce is relatively broad: to promote business through organizing domestic and international trade events and providing technical and legal advice. In addition, the chambers are increasingly keen to create a role for themselves in developing SMEs. For a firm to obtain an operating license, registration with the local chamber of commerce is mandatory. For example, the Benghazi Chamber has 36,000 registered firms. Smaller firms tend not to register. Firms tend to use the chambers mainly for assistance with licenses and legal advice because the chambers' services and support to market development and trade appear to be limited.

Private business associations also contribute to the development of the labor market, mainly through advocating for reforms to improve the business and investment climate regulations, which are overseen by the Ministry of Economy. Key issues include (a) reforming the banking sector to improve access to credit,

(b) reforming restrictive taxation policies, and (c) creating industrial zones that guarantee land availability and ownership.

Revisiting Labor Regulations

Incentives inherent in Libya's labor regulations point to areas for future assessment. The most notable of these incentives are regulations regarding (a) hiring and retention policies for nationals and non-nationals, (b) wages and benefits, and (c) unemployment benefits. Libya's *Law Number 12 for 2010 Concerning Labor Relations*, the labor code, has been under review since 2012, coupled with the drafting of a new law on labor unions.

The Libyan labor code mandates principles for entry into employment, employment contracts, and training contracts. Nevertheless, the design of the regulations, incentives, and enforcement requires a more critical assessment. In principle, employers in Libya are obligated to accept workers assigned to them by regional employment offices. The law also requires employers in both the public and private sectors to issue a formal contract to all workers. The labor code allows various contract types ranging from open-ended to fixed-term and part-time contracts (Sec. 8). However, private sector employers reportedly evade contracts with workers to avoid paying the mandatory social security contributions.

The Libyan Labor Code also stipulates that firms are obliged to accept Libyan nationals for in-house training (Sec. 81) but does not adequately specify the terms and conditions. The labor code establishes that standard working hours should not exceed 48 hours per week. The law also strictly regulates working age and has explicit protections for 16–18-year-olds. More data are needed to assess the structure and inherent incentives associated with social contributions, employer obligations, and labor market dynamics in Libya.

Several regulations effectively limit female employment, including restrictions on certain sectors and working hours (Sec. 24). Generous nonwage benefits for female workers are included in the legislation, such as prematernity and maternity leave (Sec. 25) and other family-leave entitlements. While these benefits may enable female labor force participation, additional research is needed to ascertain potential positive and negative incentives for females and employers alike arising from these regulations.

Regulations mandating how minimum wages are set and remuneration is governed are unclear, including whether minimum wages are set by sector or geographic area. Minimum wages in Libya are set by a consultative council comprising representatives from the government and representatives of trade unions and employers (Sec. 19). The 2010 labor code also stipulates automatic and annual increment and wage increases (Secs. 143–144), without setting provisions for performance. Conditions regulating overtime and remuneration are unclear. The 2010 labor code has room to clarify and introduce collective bargaining as a mechanism for setting standards in the future. The labor code allows for generous leave entitlements, including hajj, marriage, and other family entitlements (Sec. 34). These entitlements potentially incur financial and economic costs to employers. Thus, a future critical assessment is needed to review and reform these benefits to ensure that they are aligned with a vision for job creation in the private sector.

Libyan labor regulations governing dismissal generally are associated with relatively rigid requirements (Secs 42–43 of the labor code). Contract termination is subject to various steps required for employers to justify dismissal decisions. These steps are (a) review by public authorities for approval to dismiss, (b) advance notice provided the employee and public authorities, and (c) severance pay provisions.

Conclusions

Libya's institutional landscape appears to already have the main building blocks for a functional labor market. However, populating these blocks with the right strategic framework and policies to promote resilience, growth, and job creation is at stake. Supporting reforms to the business climate to facilitate investment as well as MOE's National Program for SME Development can greatly boost job creation, including support to established small enterprises. Ensuring that public financing supports a range of training and educational opportunities in the public and private sectors that enhance public sector employment services and promote public-private partnerships (PPPs) are among the key institutional MOL reforms needed.

In addition, restructuring the local chambers of commerce could help to support business development services, ideally including one-stop shops for firms and potential entrepreneurs. The chambers of commerce also have a valuable short-term role together with business leaders: to support training programs and create sector development strategies. These would help shape the policy reforms necessary to ensure implementation. A collective vision that addresses the aspirations and preferences of the labor market can be achieved. Combined with a rethink of labor legislation and empowerment of trade and labor unions, this vision can help unlock Libya's potential and promote stability.

Notes

1. World Bank. Unpublished. *Briefing Note on Governance Programs in Libya.* Unpublished.
2. World Bank, *Libya Country Economic Report 30295-LY* (Washington, DC: World Bank, 2006).
3. In 2013 approximately 400,000 people were registered as unemployed. Of these, approximately 25 percent were graduates (holding a higher education degree) and 66 percent were female.

CHAPTER 4

Profiles and Preferences of Workers: Investing in Job Training

Introduction

"Are they ready and will they accept the jobs offered?" is a question often posed in post-revolution Libya. Previous analyses of the business climate showed that 44 percent of firms believed that Libyans would not accept the types of jobs the firms offered,[1] notably in manual or semiskilled labor. Given today's overall labor market trends and the institutional landscape in Libya, designing programs and policies to gradually transform the job market begs a strategic and targeted approach. Beyond fueling economic diversification and an enabling macroeconomic environment, training, preparing, and facilitating job insertion for workers should improve how well the labor market functions, particularly for youth and combatants. Understanding the preferences, mindsets, competencies, and interactions among them; and demographics such as age, gender, and combatant profile can improve the design of labor market programs and policies to better meet the needs of the job market. Likewise, determining the quantitative trends of private sector growth, complemented by in-depth evaluations of employers' decision-making processes and the willingness to pay for investing in skills development of workers, is key to solve the riddle of labor market reforms in Libya.

This chapter evaluates how workers view the labor market outlook and examines three areas:

- *Development of a typology of job seeker profiles and new tools for doing so*. The typology describes the labor supply characteristics of different population segments and population typologies. The typology includes information on demographic profiles, current mindsets toward employment preferences and goals, levels of education, skill and work experience, and positions in and understanding of the labor market.
- *Overview of key barriers to labor market insertion*, notably questions such as "Will Libyan youth engage in practical work?" "Will Libyan youth engage in

the private sector?" and "What is required for Libyan combatants to engage in the labor market?"

- *Options for labor market entry strategies* for each population segment and population typology.

To benchmark demographic profiles, skills, and job preferences in Libya, in 2012 Bank staff used a rapid qualitative-quantitative survey to compare unemployed youth with their employed counterparts.[2] Having a higher level of education appears to be associated with full-time employment, rather than part-time or no employment (table 4.1 and table 4.2). Having at least one year of prior work experience also appears to be associated with being employed, particularly full-time (table 4.3).

The assessment was designed to sample a nearly equal proportion of employed and unemployed respondents in each location (box 4.1). However, to obtain

Table 4.1   Respondents' Employment Status by Educational Level

Employment status	Primary (%)	Secondary (%)	Tertiary (%)	Total (%)
Full-time	16	25	39	28
Part-time	11	5	7	8
Occasional	15	0	4	6
Unemployed	58	70	50	58
Total	100	100	100	100

Source: Libya Rapid Labor Market Assessment, World Bank 2012.

Table 4.2   Respondents' Employment Status by Gender

Employment status	Male (%)	Female (%)	Total (%)
Full-time	24	36	28
Part-time	7	9	8
Occasional	7	5	6
Unemployed	62	50	58
Total	100	100	100

Source: Libya Rapid Labor Market Assessment, World Bank 2012.

Table 4.3   Respondents' Employment Status by Previous Work Experience (of at least one year)

Employment status	Previous experience (%)	No previous experience (%)	Total (%)
Full-time	35	14	28
Part-time	11	0	8
Occasional	7	5	6
Unemployed	47	81	58
Total	100	100	100

Source: Libya Rapid Labor Market Assessment, World Bank 2012.

additional benchmarking profiles and skills, the assessment over-sampled employed respondents working in the private sector. As a result, the assessment reflected a lower share of public sector employment than is suggested by official statistics. In the 2012 Bank assessment, 33 percent of those sampled reported

---

Box 4.1 Design of Rapid Labor Market Assessment of Libya's Supply Side, 2012

A rapid labor market assessment survey piloting a questionnaire was conducted during July 2012. Its two purposes were (a) to complement quantitative analyses using the Libya Labor Force Surveys (LFSs) and (b) to better understand preferences and the job market outlook from the perspectives of both job seekers and employers.

The assessment was based on 67 interviews with respondents selected by location, gender, education level, and employment status, with an additional specific target group of ex-combatants. Thus, results should not be considered representative of Libya's overall situation but, rather, indicative of possible trends on the supply side of the Libyan labor market. Nearly two-thirds of the interviewees explained that they took an active part in the civil conflict. Many respondents had left their jobs due to the conflict, while some had not had the opportunity to return to their previous jobs. Therefore, the following analysis should be viewed carefully because the same assessment conducted at a different time, particularly a few months after the nomination of a new government, could yield different results.

In 2012, 58 percent of respondents were unemployed while 42 percent were employed either informally/occasionally, part-time or full-time (table B4.1.1). Of the employed respondents, more were employed part-time in Tripoli than in Misratah or Benghazi. Employees in the two latter cities were more likely to be full-time.

Of the 67 respondents, the sample comprises 45 males (67 percent) and 22 females (32 percent). Youth make up a large proportion: 45 percent were 18–24 years; 26 percent 25–29 years; 9 percent 30–34 years; and 10 percent 35 and older. In terms of educational background, 28 percent of the sample had a primary education; 30 percent, secondary education (15 percent general, 15 percent secondary vocational); and 42 percent, tertiary education (including 13.5 percent tertiary vocational). A somewhat higher proportion of males reported being unemployed than did females (62 percent versus 50 percent, respectively). More females had a tertiary education than did males: 45 percent of women sampled had a higher education degree, compared to 20 percent of men.

Table B4.1.1 Respondents' Employment Status by City

Employment status	Tripoli	Qarabuli	Misratah	Benghazi	Ajdabiyah	Zuwara	Total
Full-time (%)	17	40	36	37	0	33	28
Part-time (%)	17	0	7	0	20	0	8
Occasional (%)	6	0	7	5	20	0	6
Unemployed (%)	61	60	50	58	60	67	58
Total sample size (number)	**18**	**5**	**14**	**19**	**5**	**6**	**67**

Source: World Bank, 2012, Libya Rapid Labor Market Assessment, Washington, DC.

---

working as salaried workers in the public sector, and 30 percent in the private sector. The remainder worked as entrepreneurs (15 percent), in the nonprofit sector (11 percent), or with a *katiba*/brigade (11 percent) (figure 4.1).

Among Libyan unemployed and employed youth, social capital remains a pivotal safety net. The vast majority of interviewees acknowledge support from their families. Of these, 85 percent indicate a high level of support regarding housing and 69 percent regarding food (table 4.4). Eighty-eight percent of all job seekers live at home (table 4.4 and table 4.5). The high level of housing support reflects social norms since most Libyan youth live with their families until starting their own households, getting married, or even longer. Under the previous regime, the housing economy also may have contributed to this pattern because even though home ownership is preferred, it is a challenge for unemployed youth; and renting is considered rare. Most Libyans, therefore, tend to buy a home or live with others until they are able to buy. Housing constraints also may negatively impact labor mobility in Libya so may help explain high unemployment rates.

Fewer job seekers tend to receive direct financial assistance; 36 percent indicated a high degree of financial support. Unemployed youth indicated earning additional income through small temporary jobs or borrowing from friends.

Employment Preferences

Most job seekers primarily seek public sector jobs: 75 percent of respondents indicated that they were highly eager to enter the civil service (figure 4.2). Sixty-seven percent of respondents indicated that their main reasons for preferring a

Figure 4.1 Primary Occupations among Employed Respondents by Type (percent)

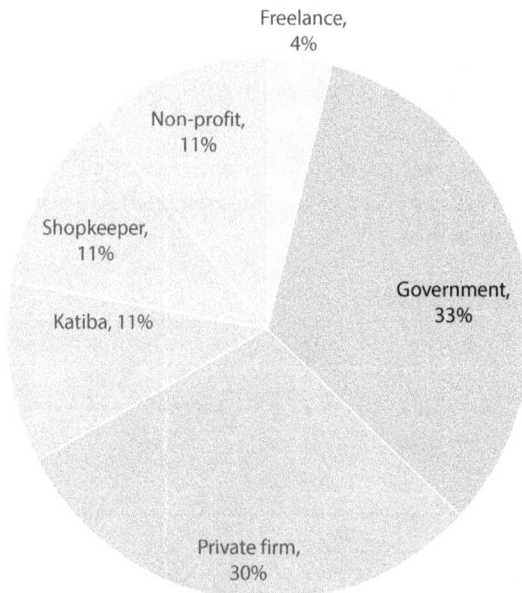

Source: Libya Rapid Labor Market Assessment, World Bank 2012.

Table 4.4 Respondents, Receiving Family Support by Type and Level

Level of support	Financial (%)	Housing (%)	Food (%)
High	36	85	69
Medium/Occasional	19	6	16
Low/None	45	9	15
Total	100	100	100

Source: Libya Rapid Labor Market Assessment, World Bank 2012.

Table 4.5 Respondents' Living Arrangements by Marital Status

Marital status	Live with parents (%)	Own home (%)	Rent home (%)	Total (%)
Single/engaged	93	0	0	82
Married (with/without children)	7	100	100	18
Total	88	9	3	100

Source: Libya Rapid Labor Market Assessment, World Bank 2012.

Figure 4.2 Level of Job Search Interest by Job Type Preference

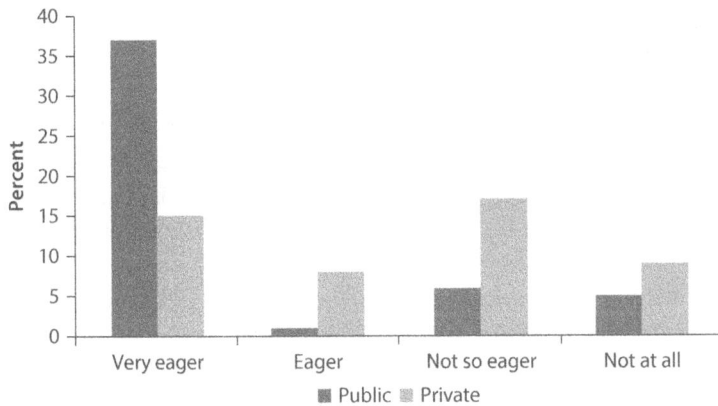

Source: Libya Rapid Labor Market Assessment, World Bank 2012.
Note: n=49.

civil service position were job security, benefits such as pensions, and easier access to bank loans. Some respondents also indicated that positions within the public sector are "more comfortable": they are often "nine-to-five" jobs with a limited workload and a broad flexibility regarding actual presence at work. Conversely, for the few who did not want to work as civil servants, the main reason cited was salary, which they perceived to be lower in the public service.

Most job seekers consider private sector employment to be unstable. Only 17 percent preferred employment in the private sector over the public sector (figure 4.3). Except for a minority of respondents, the private sector was perceived to be less secure, less likely to pay well in the long term, and less likely

Figure 4.3   Job Search Preferences by Job Type

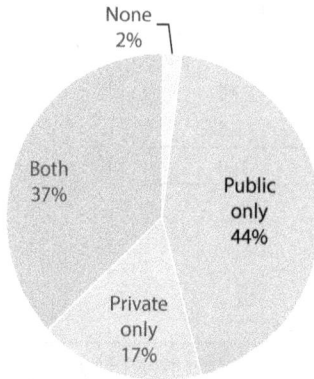

Source: Libya Rapid Labor Market Assessment, World Bank 2012.
Note: n=49.

to provide social security benefits than the public sector. However, employment in foreign firms remained of interest to many job seekers. Several respondents mentioned that they would work for foreign private firms, which they perceived to pay and treat workers better and provide benefits.

Skills

The assessment included a rapid self-evaluation of skills and competencies. Respondents provided their own perceptions of their skill strengths, weaknesses, and future training interests. Performing an objective evaluation of respondents' skills would have required rigorous survey techniques, which was outside the scope of this initial assessment (box 4.2). Skills were included that represented cognitive, noncognitive, and technical skills (including job-specific skills). The questionnaire asked respondents to rate their skills on a scale of 0–10, using a 10-point Likert scale, which provides useful baseline information for designing a broader assessment in the future. This approach does not provide an external, objective assessment of their skills but, rather, a perspective based on their views and preferences. The results showed that respondents exhibited a wide variation in responses and thus exhibited a limited bias. Thus, the findings can be used as a good basis for an initial understanding of the skills gap.

Skills perceived by job seekers as most valuable for competing in the labor market were both noncognitive and cognitive skills, followed by technical and job-specific skills. Respondents cited basic information technology (IT) (25 percent of respondents), foreign languages (18 percent), planning and organizing (8 percent), and oral communication (8 percent). Respondents also considered themselves weakest at these skills, including foreign languages and information technology (IT), followed by management, communication, and numeracy (figure 4.4).

Box 4.2   Future Directions for Assessing Employment Skills

Prior to designing any policies for skills development and training, to address any mismatch, gaining a clear understanding of skill supply and demand is necessary. This understanding can be achieved through a labor market assessment that analyzes the capacities of the labor force and matches them against marketplace demand. Such an assessment will enable the government to go beyond matching educational attainments and trainings to monitoring and analysis of the distribution of skills in different sectors among Libya's working age population.

Labor force skills that usually are assessed include cognitive; personality; family background; and, depending on the tool, technical skills. Two prominent tools designed for this purpose are the Skills toward Employment and Productivity (STEP) measurement study, operated by the World Bank, and the Program for the International Assessment of Adult Competencies (PIAAC), operated by Organisation for Economic Co-Operation and Development (OECD). International assessments such as these enable cross-country comparisons and benchmarking against countries with similar contexts for the ultimate goal of identifying potential lessons learned.

Source: World Bank staff.

Figure 4.4   Average Self-Rated Score by Skill Level among Libyan Job Seekers

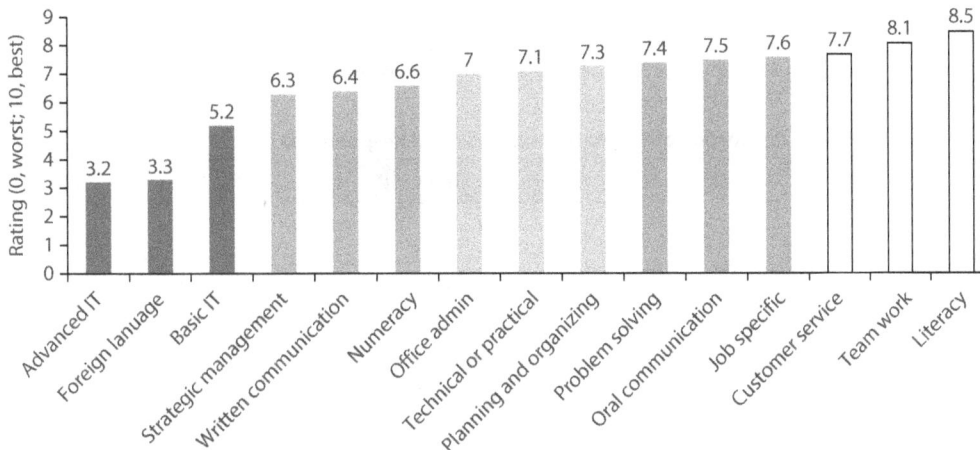

Source: World Bank, 2012, Libya Rapid Labor Market Assessment, Washington, DC.
Note: IT = information technology.

In contrast, respondents tended to rate their technical skills, including literacy, numeracy, and job-specific skills, relatively highly. Most respondents indicated that they wanted to improve their skills in foreign languages (54 percent), followed by basic IT (40 percent) and advanced IT (25 percent). Following graduation from secondary or tertiary school, job seekers tend to enroll most frequently in training programs to upgrade their skills in basic IT (47 percent) and foreign languages (29 percent).

Employed respondents appear to rate certain skills more highly than the average level of all respondents, including basic IT, problem solving, literacy, office administration, and technical and practical skills (table 4.6 and table 4.7). Although the sample is too small to draw robust comparisons, these findings shed

Table 4.6   Distribution of Respondents' Skills by Level

Skills/Rating	High (%)	Medium (%)	Low (%)	Average value (rating)
Advanced IT	7	26	67	**3.2**
Foreign language	10	23	66	**3.3**
Basic IT	31	28	42	**5.2**
Strategic management	44	27	29	**6.3**
Written communication	43	34	23	**6.4**
Numeracy	38	48	14	**6.6**
Office admin	59	20	21	**7.0**
Technical or practical	52	31	18	**7.1**
Planning and organizing	56	32	11	**7.3**
Problem solving	54	35	11	**7.4**
Oral communication	57	29	14	**7.5**
Job specific	67	25	8	**7.6**
Customer service	61	30	9	**7.7**
Team work	71	22	6	**8.1**
Literacy	75	19	6	**8.5**

Source: World Bank, 2012, Libya Rapid Labor Market Assessment, Washington, DC.

Table 4.7   Proportion of Self-Rated Highly Skilled Respondents (%)

Skills	Full-time employed (%)	All respondents (%)
Basic IT	47	39
Advanced IT	11	8
Oral communication	79	75
Written communication	58	52
Customer service	74	70
Team work	84	84
Foreign language	16	17
Problem solving	79	64
Planning	63	63
Strategic management	58	55
Numeracy	47	50
Literacy	90	80
Office admin	84	70
Technical/practical	79	67
Job specific	74	69

Source: World Bank, 2012, Libya Rapid Labor Market Assessment, Washington, DC.
Note: "Highly skilled" indicates respondents with a self-rated score of at least 8 on a scale of 1 to 10.

light on areas for further evaluation. Interestingly, these results do not distinguish the foreign language skills of the employed and average respondents. The reason may be that most of the employed respondents (approximately 56 percent) either work for the public sector or are part of a brigade.

Job Search

Libyans tend to search for and find jobs through personal networks. The majority of job seekers (72 percent) indicated that they were job hunting through word of mouth, 20 percent through the internet,[3] 19 percent through Ministry of Labor and Manpower (MOL), and 15 percent by sending unsolicited applications to potential employers. However, employment services provided by MOL generally are perceived as inefficient. A sizable proportion of job seekers had registered with MOL services (35 percent), only one had received a job referral from MOL but it did not lead to employment. In addition, 30 percent of respondents had registered with Warriors Affairs Commission (WAC), but only three received job referrals. Others were either waiting for results to come or believed the whole process was unsuccessful. Overall, job seekers had greater awareness of the unemployment services provided by WAC (66 percent) than those provided by MOL (46 percent). This finding may suggest that WAC's outreach efforts are more effective than MOL's.

The perceived ease of finding employment and job preference varies by gender, with more females than males reporting the need to find a nonmanual job. Thirty percent of females perceived that it could be easier for males than for females to find jobs, stating that, for example, males may be perceived as more available. The greatest barrier mentioned by female job seekers was the perceived lack of preferred jobs and/or job conditions. A preferred job was deemed to be a nonmanual job (such as a waitress or housekeeper) in an environment in which women would not be potentially subject to harassment and from which they could leave early enough to return home before nightfall. Another important barrier mentioned was family constraints, whether household or children responsibilities; or a perceived lack of support for working from husbands or parents. Only 2 of the 17 female job seekers perceived no barriers to finding a job.

Most combatants in this assessment indicated that they identified and anticipated jobs that would come through in the near future, or were fully employed with the katiba. Of the 16 combatants, 90 percent (15 of 16) were unemployed.[4] Active combatants ranged from 22–37 years old, with 30 percent having completed primary education, 30 having completed secondary education, and 40 percent having completed tertiary education. Eighty-two percent had had previous work experience, typically in manual jobs (that is, cleaner, worker at a petrol station, salesperson, or taxi driver). Eight are working full-time for their katiba; two prefer to stay involved in security forces (police or army); three expressed a preference for returning to education; three for finding a job; and one for entrepreneurship.

Typology of Job Seeker Profiles

Libyan job seekers were found to fall into one of eight profiles (figure 4.5). Each profile bears certain preferences and needs for job insertion. Such a typology helps in designing and targeting employment and training programs, as well as in preparing reforms to improve workforce development and the education system. The typology of profiles is based on analyzing and grouping key characteristics of the unemployed (box 4.3).

Active, unemployed job seekers make up 15 percent of the unemployed in the assessment. They are largely graduates with no prior work experience who have submitted several job applications over the past two months. They tend to come from lower income households (that is, below 880 LYD per household per month, compared to an average 1,360 LYD per household per month). Typically, these job seekers are registered at MOL and WAC. Although they have a preference for nonmanual, professional jobs, they likely are willing to accept manual service jobs (such as cashiers and waiters). However, their job-seeking methods usually are not rigorous. Applying for a job often is understood as phoning other individuals to see whether they are aware of job openings, and many have not circulated an updated curriculum vita (CV). However, this category tends to be highly motivated due in part to limited household income and in part to being relatively highly skilled. They likely would benefit from job coaching and would be candidates for a job-matching service.

Figure 4.5 Job Seeker Profiles among the Unemployed

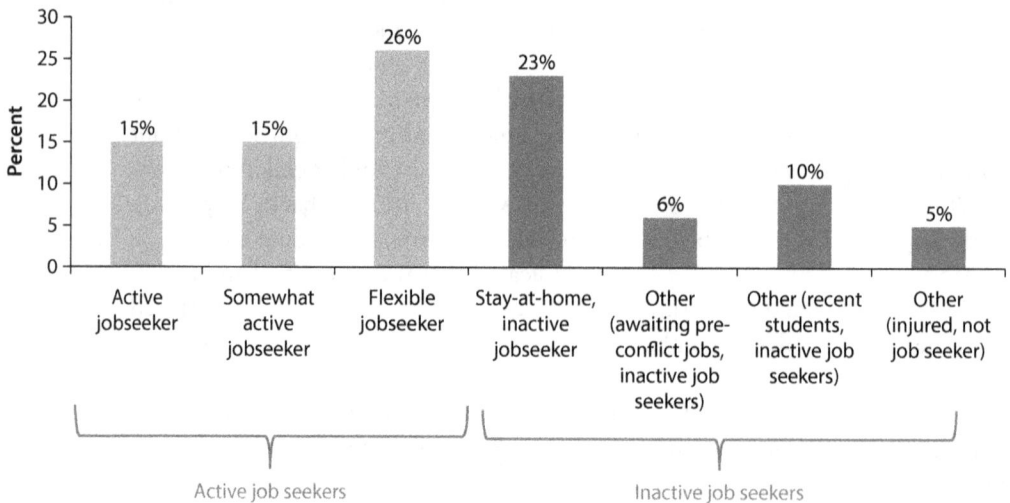

Source: Libya Rapid Labor Market Assessment, World Bank 2012.

Box 4.3 Methodology for Developing Job Seeker Profiles

A profile of different types of job seekers was developed to understand the type of jobs and preferences sought by different groups. Of approximately 350 variables collected during the assessment, 12 dimensions were deemed the most relevant to understand the various types of job seekers in Libya. A statistical analysis known as 2-step clustering was performed on these variables to identify 10 distinctive typologies. The dimensions used to develop the typology are:

- **Employment status**: Employed full-time, under-employed (part-time or much lower than their theoretical level), unemployed
- **Gender**
- **Age group**
- **Location**: City
- **Job-seeking status**: Based on the number of times that the person has submitted an application in the past two months, and the type and methods for looking for a job
- **Previous work experience**: Based on employment history. Respondents who had more than one year of relevant work experience were considered to have previous work experience.
- **Education level**: Primary, secondary (general or vocational), tertiary education
- **Vocational training**: Whether the applicant has had vocational training
- **Skills**: Self-rated level of various skills
- **Family support**: Level of financial, housing, or food support received from family members
- **Willingness to take manual or technical jobs**
- **Willingness to take manual service jobs** (waiters, cashiers).

Source: Libya Rapid Labor Market Assessment, World Bank 2012.

Somewhat active job seekers comprise 15 percent of the unemployed who are long-term unemployed (at least six months) and believe that they can find a job without the need for job support or active job-seeking activities. Job seekers in this category tend to be males who have some previous work experience and are searching intermittently for a job. They tend to live with and depend on their families for support. Typically, they have a secondary education but are not interested in manual labor or manual service jobs because they perceive these jobs to be physically demanding. Due to the perception of a stable salary and job security, their preference lies with public sector employment.

However, they also would like to open their own businesses, such as small shops in retail or goods (car sales, coffee shops, jewelry stores). At the same time, they have not prepared plans and assume that they would not have the necessary funds. These job seekers assume that the most likely jobs available for them would be administrative positions or mid-level management, but do not have a clear idea of where to find information about openings. They have not registered with MOL, and only half of them have registered with WAC. They likely have not been involved as combatants, and if so, may have had a logistics role and who may continue to be members of a katiba. These job seekers are particularly interested in the public sector and greater access to financing and loans for small and medium enterprise (SME) creation, but may benefit from reconversion vocational training.

Flexible job seekers, comprising 26 percent of the unemployed, are willing to take nearly any jobs, including manual jobs. They tend to come from households with a lower than average income (679 LYD per month compared to an average in the sample of 1,363 LYD per month). Their preferred jobs included electrician, carpenter, factory operator, or construction operator (7 of 9); mechanic (6 of 9); and shop assistant, salesperson, or cashier (5 of 10). The least preferred jobs were street cleaner (1 of 10); construction worker (2 of 10); farm worker or plumber (3 of 10); and painter, waiter, and housekeeper (4 of 10). This group would be a strong candidate for vocational training and apprenticeship programs.

Stay-at-home, inactive job seekers account for 23 percent of the unemployed. They comprise largely unemployed married women and, to a smaller extent, single women. This group includes women who are married and have decided not to work (78 percent), as well as women who are single and have expressed wanting to get married before working (22 percent). Some have had temporary jobs while studying. Two job seekers indicated that they would be interested in finding jobs and had registered with MOL but are not actively conducting job searches beyond registration.

Other inactive job seekers, including recent graduates and workers waiting to return to pre-conflict jobs, comprise 10 percent and 5 percent of the unemployed, respectively. These categories do not conform to a particular profile. Four individuals (including two combatants) had already applied for jobs and were involved in the application process. At the time of the interview, one individual was completing paperwork to join the police force. One had just started work as a mobile phone application developer; and two were planning to return to their pre-conflict jobs at firms whose activities had been interrupted during the conflict. Four respondents, including two combatants and two women, were recent graduates and said they would either continue their education or actively seek jobs in the near future. Another two individuals, comprising 5 percent of the unemployed, had been physically injured during the conflict so were unable to work.

Underemployed job seekers comprise 8 percent of all respondents and tend to be informally employed in temporary jobs with an average duration of less than six months. They typically have a primary or secondary school educations and come from low- or middle-income households. Underemployed, continuous job

Figure 4.6   Self-Reported Income (LYD per Month) by Gender

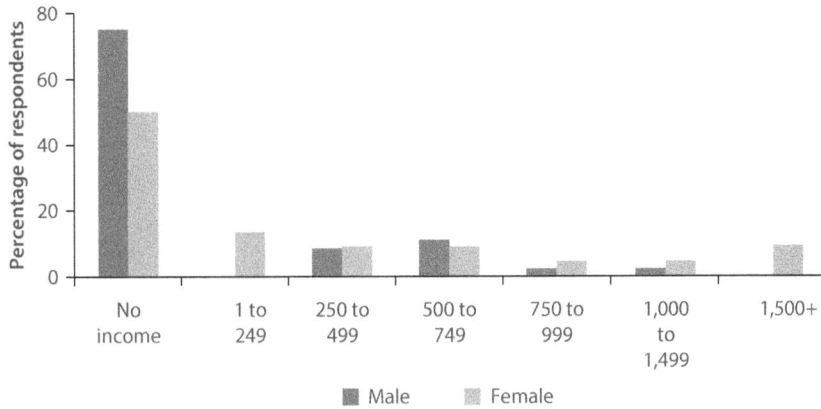

Source: World Bank, 2012, Libya Rapid Labor Market Assessment, Washington, DC.

seekers tend to be employed in retail or services and are less interested in taking manual jobs. These job seekers are more highly represented in Misratah and Benghazi than in the western regions. This group tends to prefer jobs with the government for job security and stability. Given that this group has had some previous work experience, individuals in this group would benefit from apprenticeship and skills upgrade programs.

Employed, full-time job seekers make up 22 percent of all respondents and occasionally are searching for a job. They tend to have a higher education level than the average job seeker in the sample and are less interested in manual jobs. Of the eight job seekers in this category, four individuals work for private firms, two for nonprofit organizations, and two for the government. They report wages ranging from 280 to 1,500 LYD per month (figure 4.6). In this sample, the average salary reported by females is somewhat higher than that reported by males (580 LYD per month versus 450 LYD per month, respectively).

Conclusions

Complementing labor force statistics, important factors linked to finding gainful employment in Libya include motivation, household support, and personal networks. Based on an in-depth assessment, three categories of job seekers appear to represent the majority of job seekers: active job seekers, underemployed job seekers, and job seekers who are employed full time but are looking to find better employment. In the short term, there is an opportunity to support the three primary categories of job seekers with policies and programs for firm-based job training, job-coaching programs, and job-seeking services through the public and/ or private sector. Strengthening professional, cognitive, and noncognitive skills beyond IT and languages will be critical and best achieved through strong partnerships with private sector firms.

Notes

1. World Bank, *Libya 2010 Investment Climate Assessment* (Washington, DC: World Bank, 2011).
2. World Bank, *Libya Rapid Labor Market Assessment* (Washington, DC: World Bank, 2012).
3. Job seekers cited using the following Libyan websites for their job search: www.libya-ninvestment.com, www.ly.opensooq.com, and www.jobs.ly.
4. Another 52 percent (35 respondents) indicated they had "participated" in the conflict but were not considered combatants.

CHAPTER 5

Perspectives of Firms: Investing in the Business Climate

Introduction

As part of this report, the assessment also evaluated the six economic sectors likely representing those with the greatest job creation potential to reveal the business climate and skills barriers to creating growth and employment. The sectors assessed were manufacturing construction, trade, services, hospitality, and agriculture/fisheries. Although the Libyan private sector had started to show signs of recovery prior to 2014, many foreign firms left Libya at the start of the revolution. State-owned enterprises (SOEs) tend to be fully staffed yet barely operational, in large part due to political uncertainty. To evaluate the needs and perspectives of employers (box 5.1), this chapter evaluates three areas:

- *Development of a typology of economic sectors and firms*, including job creation perspectives; employment profiles; and skills demand in small, medium, and large enterprises
- *Options for short- to medium-term labor absorption strategies* for certain sectors and firms
- *Overview of key barriers to labor market absorption*, including questions such as "Will enterprises in Libya employ Libyans?", "Can small enterprises in Libya benefit from national development programs?", and "What is the willingness to pay of firms to invest in training of workers, either in-house or externally?"

Growth and Employment

Oil and gas extraction dominates Libya's economy. The sector contributed approximately 54 percent of gross domestic product (GDP) in 2011 but decreased during 2012–13 as a result of political instability. Other productive nonoil and gas sectors are small in comparison. The next largest are construction (8.7 percent), real estate and professional activities (7.1 percent), and manufacturing (6.9 percent) (figure 5.1). Compounding the two issues of declining oil

Box 5.1   Design of Rapid Labor Market Assessment of the Demand Side

As part of this report, the rapid assessment evaluated 61 Libyan firms selected based on location, sector, and ownership (public or private) (table B5.1.1). Thirty-eight firms were based in Tripoli, 13 in Misratah, and 10 in Benghazi. Approximately 10 firms were interviewed per sector, which were manufacturing, construction, trade, services, hospitality, and agriculture and fishing. Forty-nine of the firms were private, and 12 were state owned. Size range also was taken into account: small (fewer than 20 employees), medium (20–100 employees), and large (over 100 employees) firms were selected. The 61 firms interviewed employed a total of 13,786 people, with a median number of 31 employees per firm. Firm size ranged from 3 employees (footwear repair firm) to 1,930 employees (cement firm).

Table B5.1.1   Sectors Assessed by Total Number of Firms and Employees

Sector	No. of firms	Total no. of employees
Manufacturing	10	4,719
Construction	10	2,300
Trade	8	2,185
Services	12	1,990
Hospitality	13	1,785
Agriculture/fishery	8	807
Total	**61**	**13,786**

Source: World Bank, 2012, Libya Rapid Labor Market Assessment, Washington, DC.
Note: Total number of unfilled jobs was 341, for a total of 14,127 jobs.

Figure 5.1   Sectoral Contribution to GDP, 2011

US$ million/year, percent

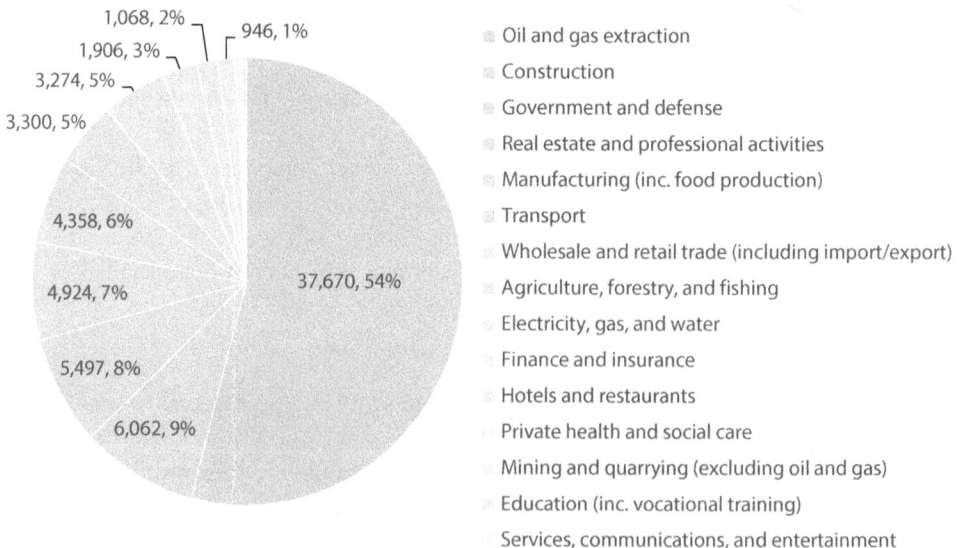

- Oil and gas extraction
- Construction
- Government and defense
- Real estate and professional activities
- Manufacturing (inc. food production)
- Transport
- Wholesale and retail trade (including import/export)
- Agriculture, forestry, and fishing
- Electricity, gas, and water
- Finance and insurance
- Hotels and restaurants
- Private health and social care
- Mining and quarrying (excluding oil and gas)
- Education (inc. vocational training)
- Services, communications, and entertainment

Pie chart values: 1,068, 2%; 1,906, 3%; 3,274, 5%; 3,300, 5%; 4,358, 6%; 4,924, 7%; 5,497, 8%; 6,062, 9%; 37,670, 54%; 946, 1%

Source: Central Bank of Libya data, 2011.
Note: GDP = gross domestic product.

and gas revenues due to political upheavals and no close productive competitors is that no other sector can match the oil and gas sector in salaries, training, and international exposure.

Compared to other sectors, employment opportunities in the oil and gas sector are limited (table 5.1). This sector employs only approximately 40,000 Libyans. This report considers that, due to the sector's requirements for highly skilled staff in remote locations, its short-term labor absorption capacity (other than a few internships at the headquarters) is rather limited. In the longer term, regardless of any unforeseen major new investments and alterations to the labor law, oil and gas extraction growth rates are likely to hover around the 6 percent achieved in 2009. This growth likely translates into approximately 1,000 new jobs annually, probably attracting the brightest and best of Libya's job seekers.

Table 5.1   Active Labor Force by Economic Sector in Libya, 2011

Sector	2010 GDP (US$ million/yr)	2010 GDP Share (% of GDP)	2008–09 Nominal Growth (%)	Employment (000s)	Employment Share (% of active labor force)
Oil and gas extraction	37,670	54.1	6.2	40,000	3
Construction	6,062	8.7	26.4	35,000	3
Government and defense	5,497	7.9	3.0	790,000	57
Real estate and professional activities[a]	4,924	7.1	7.5	20,000	1
Manufacturing (including food production)	4,358	6.3	11.4	50,000	4
Transport[a]	3,300	4.7	6.2	25,000	2
Wholesale and retail trade (including import/export)	3,274	4.7	8.8	80,000	6
Agriculture, forestry, and fishing[b]	1,906	2.7	6.0	19,000	1
Electricity, gas, and water	1,068	1.5	10.9	50,000	3.6
Finance and insurance[a]	946	1.4	9.3	15,000	1
Hotels and restaurants[a]	164	0.2	9.0	15,000	1
Private health and social care[a]	132	0.2	5.8	15,000	1
Mining and quarrying (excluding oil and gas)[a]	115	0.2	12.5	5,000	0.4
Education (including vocational training)[a]	107	0.2	9.8	200,000	14.5
Services, communication, and entertainment[a]	73	0.1	11.0	20,000	1.5
Total	**69,596**	**100**		**1,379,000**	**100**

Source: Sector size and growth: Central Bank of Libya, Q4 2010 data. Employment per sector: Libyan Agency for Statistics, 2010 data.
Note: Employment reflects Libyan nationals.
a. Authors' estimates for employment.
b. Other reports indicate employment in agriculture is 9.4 percent. However, this estimate likely includes foreign labor.

Outside of the public sector education and defense sectors, wholesale and retail employ the largest workforce of approximately 80,000 Libyans. Past years have shown nominal sector growth of approximately 8 percent, slightly higher than nominal national GDP growth (approximately 6 percent in 2010). However, post-revolution growth has been high, with 70 percent of the 4,200 new firms registered in Tripoli in the first six months of 2012 applying for an import-export license.[1] If this situation is mirrored in Benghazi and Misratah, Libya's second and third largest labor markets, it is likely that 5,000–10,000 new jobs already may have been created. Moreover, there is high potential for strong future employment growth because domestic consumption generally is expected to increase through improved distribution of oil wealth.

In the medium term (within two years), the construction sector likely will be an important source of employment. The sector employs approximately only 35,000 Libyans, but nominal growth just before the revolution was extremely high, at approximately 26 percent annually. In the short term, growth will be moderate because many of the larger government-sponsored projects are on hold until the political situation stabilizes. The General Projects Committee (GPC), a division of the Ministry of Housing and Infrastructure, reported that, of the 12,000 construction projects in progress just before the uprising, only 400 were progressing in 2012. In the longer term, however, the construction component of new national development strategies well may drive the construction sector once again, add possibly up to 4,000 jobs per year. If vocational training schemes can start to replace elements of foreign labor on the larger construction projects, the labor absorption capacity of the construction sector could rise even further.

Likewise, the manufacturing sector is expected to contribute substantially to job creation. Employing 50,000 Libyans, the sector has benefited from a recent government diversification strategy. This strategy likely has contributed to a strong nominal growth of approximately 11 percent, which could translate into approximately 3,000 new jobs annually. Food manufacture stands out as a particular growth opportunity. Libya imports 75 percent of its food requirements.[2] The country does not even process for export any notable quantities of dates, olives, or fish, all of which are harvested in exportable qualities and quantities. Start-ups in this subsector could benefit from lower capital requirements when compared with other subsectors such as oil and gas component manufacture.

The contribution to job growth by state-owned enterprises and small, medium, and large enterprises varies by sector. In construction, the larger contracts typically are managed by state construction-implementing agencies such as the Organization for Development of Administrative Centers (ODAC) and the Housing and Investment Board (HIB). Firms that implement projects often are subsidiaries of the Economic and Social Development Fund (ESDF). These firms typically operate through partnerships with large foreign firms, which often bring in their own foreign labor forces. Growth in the construction sector is expected to come through the creation of smaller Libyan construction firms that are contracted for nongovernmental projects or subcontracted by larger firms. The larger firms may not themselves take on many laborers but rather may employ managers.

The wholesale and retail sector in Libya comprises mainly micro and small informal private firms.[3] Post-revolution growth in this sector appears to be following this trend. However, in the medium term, the expected entrance of large foreign supermarket chains may alter the sector. Manufacturing appears to be split between smaller private manufacturing firms typically producing construction-related materials (such as building blocks or fabricated structures),[4] and larger state manufacturing firms producing commodities such as petrochemicals, cement, steel, and flour as well as some specialty items (fruit juices, cigarettes, bicycles).

Despite uncertainty regarding the pace of economic recovery, most firms indicated that they expected positive growth over the next six months and accelerated growth over two years. Forty-four percent of firms reported having lost employees due to the conflict. Nevertheless, in 2012 the majority of firms reported having recovered following the conflict, with the exception of firms in the construction sector (figure 5.2). Seventy percent of firms in the construction sector reported not having recovered at all, followed by trade (38 percent) and manufacturing (31 percent). Despite the impact of the conflict, 75 percent of firms felt positive about growth over the coming six months, particularly in the services sector (media, legal, information technology [IT]) and food manufacturing (figure 5.3). Eighty-two percent of firms had believed that growth would accelerate within two years, the conflict as of 2014 notwithstanding. The manufacturing and service sectors were the most optimistic (80 percent and 73 percent, respectively). The construction sector remained the most negative, with

Figure 5.2 Libya's Level of Economic Recovery Relative to Pre-Conflict Growth by Sector

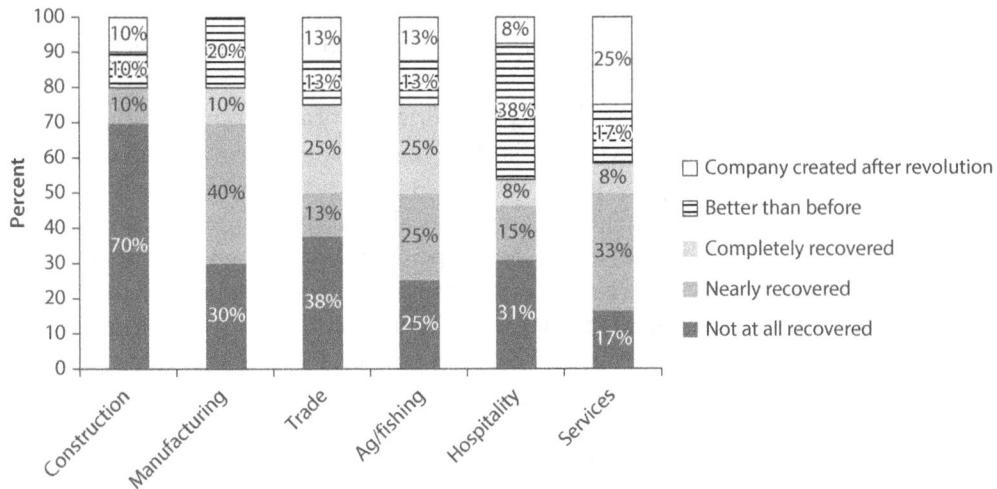

Source: World Bank, 2012, Libya Rapid Labor Market Assessment, Washington, DC.

Figure 5.3 Perspectives of Growth over six Months versus two Years

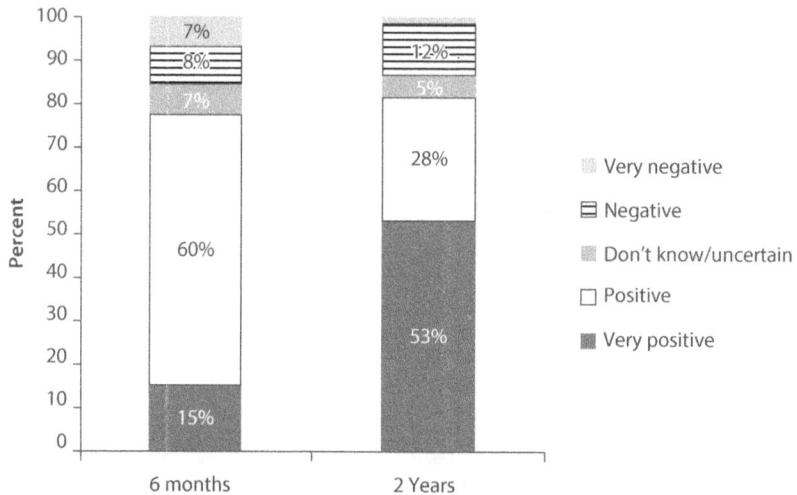

Source: World Bank, 2012, Libya Rapid Labor Market Assessment, Washington, DC.

30 percent of firms expecting negative growth over the next two years. Reasons cited for negative growth perspectives included restrictive trade regulations, a lack of contract issuance for public-private enterprises (notably in the construction sector), and emerging competition.

Firms expect job creation to accelerate, with 45 percent of firms planning to create jobs within six months. In 2012 an estimated total of 600 jobs was expected to be created, or a rate of employment growth of 6.3 percent, over a six-month period (figure 5.3 and figure 5.4). The most jobs were expected to be the hospitality sector (250), followed by trade (150), and manufacturing (100). However, firms largely felt that immediate openings would be filled by foreign workers, with only 27 percent expected to be filled by Libyan nationals (in hospitality, construction, and SOEs).

Regarding the business climate, most firms advocate reforms to simplify procedures and increase access to financial and business services, including skills development for entrepreneurs. Most firms are registered with 1 of the 14 local Chambers of Commerce (CoC) and/or local business associations. Seventy percent were registered with a CoC and 23 percent with business associations. Most of the latter firms comprise private construction, manufacturing, and trade firms. The CoC is used primarily for licensing, registration, and, to a much lesser extent, tax and contract advice (figure 5.5). Most notably, 16 percent of firms called for reforms to simplify bureaucracy, particularly for hiring foreign labor and registering firms. Other recommendations included greater access to financing, technical and legal advice, and training.

Figure 5.4 Perspectives of Growth over the Next Six Months by Sector

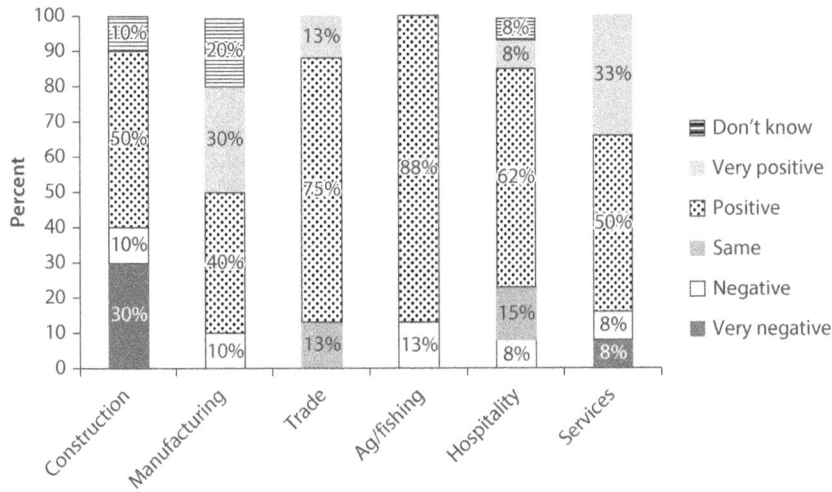

Source: World Bank, 2012, Libya Rapid Labor Market Assessment, Washington, DC.

Figure 5.5 Libyan Firms' Demands for Services from Chambers of Commerce, 2012

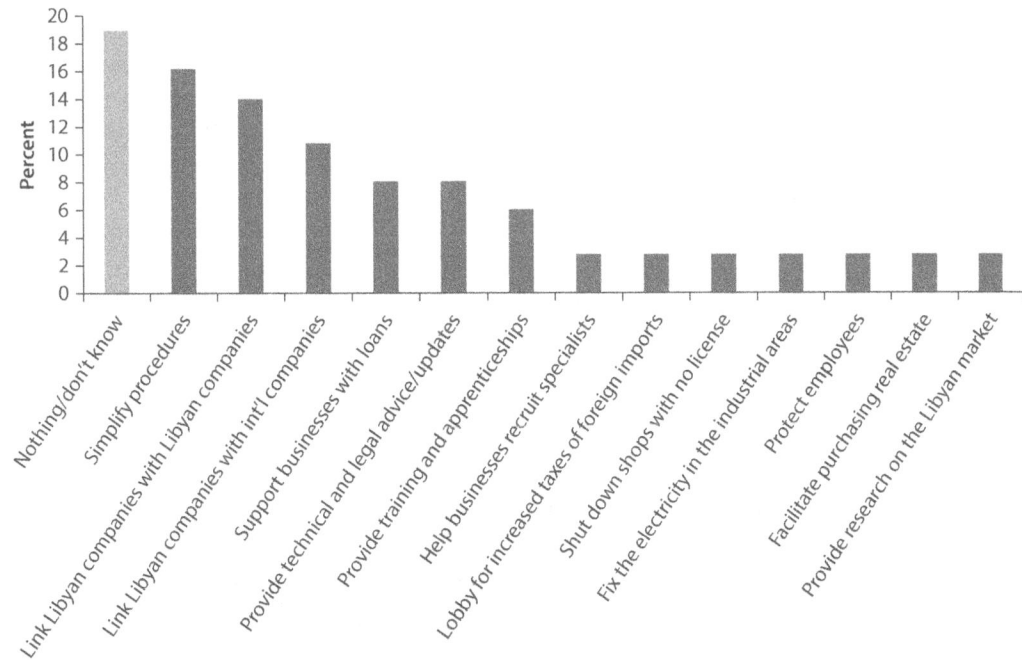

Source: World Bank, 2012, Libya Rapid Labor Market Assessment, Washington, DC.

Hiring Practices for National and Foreign Workers

Following the revolution, the vast majority of workers employed in the private sector and state-owned enterprises were Libyan. An estimated 1 million foreign workers had left during the conflict. Of a total of 13,786 workers employed by the assessed firms in 2012, 94 percent were Libyan. Prior to the revolution, these firms estimated that an average of 90 percent of their workforce had been Libyan and 10 percent foreign. Therefore, given that foreign workers made up an estimated 40 percent of the total labor force (informal and formal sectors), the vast majority of foreign workers who left Libya likely had been working in the informal sector.

As expected, the assessment shows that the share of foreign workers is three times as high in the private sector as in SOEs. The firm whose workforce comprises the largest share of foreign workers is a dairy firm (17 percent, or 100 of a total of 600 staff during low season). Foreign workers comprise 14 percent of the work force in the hospitality sector, 11 percent in agriculture and fishing, 3 percent in construction and 1 percent in services. The majority of foreign workers (85 percent) are from countries in the Middle East and North Africa, 15 percent from Nigeria, and 10 percent from Bangladesh. Among Middle East and North Africa and neighboring countries, 48 percent are from the Arab Republic of Egypt, 28 percent from Tunisia, 21 percent from Sudan, and 20 percent from Morocco.

Foreign workers in the private sector tend to fill semi- and highly technical jobs in manufacturing and engineering. Seventy-two percent of firms reported that foreign laborers work as technicians or process operatives, the most common job for foreign workers cited, followed by elementary jobs (day laborers) (figure 5.6). Foreign workers also are employed in highly skilled or professional positions, although only 17 percent of firms employ foreign workers as managers. This pattern appears similar across sectors.

Most firms perceive that Libyan workers tend not to accept manual, low-skilled jobs, and express difficulty in filling highly skilled jobs due to a lack of skills. At the time of the assessment, 341 vacancies were being advertised, equivalent to nearly 2.4 percent of all unfilled jobs. Firms consider it difficult to find required highly skilled candidates required for certain positions, particularly in services. At the same time, they tend to view visa procedures for hiring foreign nationals as being overly complex and barriers to hiring more foreign workers.

The most common approach used by firms to recruit workers is through personal networks, cited by 80 percent of firms. Forty percent of firms advertise job openings directly and 20 percent recruit workers through Ministry of Labor (MOL). MOL is used most often by large SOEs and firms looking to hire foreign nationals. Of those firms who advertise job openings, more tend to advertise online, followed by traditional media (print and radio).

Figure 5.6 Libyan Firms Reporting Hiring Nationals versus Foreign Workers by Occupation

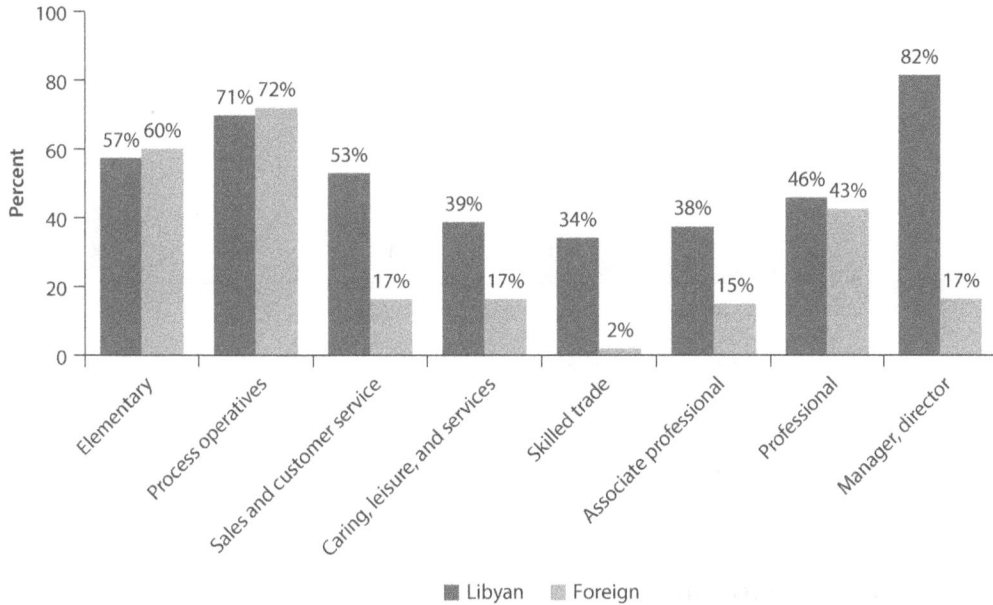

Source: World Bank, 2012, Libya Rapid Labor Market Assessment, Washington, DC.

Contracts

The majority of firms report offering relatively short-term contracts particularly in the private sector, ranging from six months (among 10 firms, or 18 percent of firms) to one year (among 25 firms, or 45 percent) (figure 5.6). This pattern contributes to high turnover, particularly in the hospitality sector (31 percent employees are reported to stay six months or less), services (25 percent), and manufacturing (20 percent). Libyan labor legislation requires that a contract be established between employers and employees, but firms seem reluctant to offer longer term contracts or to renew contracts of workers who do not perform. Among the latter, reasons cited by firms include low productivity and/or a lack of skills such as commitment to working hours and promptness.

Smaller firms in the private sector have a harder time retaining workers. Overall, 52 percent of private firms consider it difficult to retain Libyan nationals, compared to 25 percent among SOEs (figure 5.7). Smaller firms have greater difficulty retaining workers (50 percent) compared to larger firms (20 percent), reflecting the more comprehensive benefits packages[5] and relatively longer contracts offered by the latter. A higher proportion of firms in the service sector report the difficulty of retaining staff (58 percent), followed by trade, construction, agriculture and fishery, and hospitality (38 percent).

Figure 5.7   Ease of Retention of Libyan Nationals by Economic Sector, Size, and Type of Firm

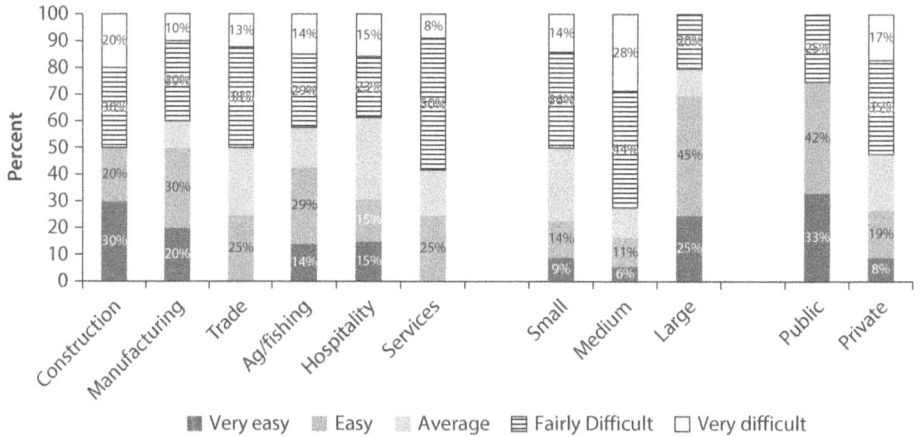

Source: World Bank, 2012, Libya Rapid Labor Market Assessment, Washington, DC.

Skills and Training

Prior work experience increases the likelihood that firms will express interest in hiring candidates, regardless of educational level. Skills and hiring prospects were assessed in terms of educational background, work experience, and specific competencies. Forty-two percent of firms would recruit a candidate with a secondary education but no prior work experience, which increases to 65 percent for the same candidate who has had prior work experience. Firms indicated that previous work experience of at least one to three years bolstered confidence in candidates.

The emphasis on education and previous work experience varies greatly by sector and firm. Fifty-seven percent of firms in sectors dominated by manual jobs (restaurant work, carpentry, food processing, tire repair) indicated that they do not use education or work experience as hiring criteria. Rather, these firms rely more heavily on on-the-job training specific to their sectors. The remaining firms which require non-manual labor tend to value work experience highly, particularly for consulting positions, legal advisors, and manufacturing jobs, where more than six years of prior work experience often is needed. Most firms expressed the need for basic IT, foreign languages, advanced IT, and technical and practical skills (figure 5.8).

More advanced noncognitive skills such as team work, problem solving, and planning are the next most desired. Firms indicated that the most difficult skills to find in candidates were foreign languages and basic and advanced IT (figure 5.9).

The majority of firms indicated that they offered on-the-job induction and certified training programs for employees. Seventy-four percent of firms offer internships or apprenticeships. Eighty-five percent provide in-house induction or

Figure 5.8 Likelihood of Recruitment by Level of Education and Previous Work Experience

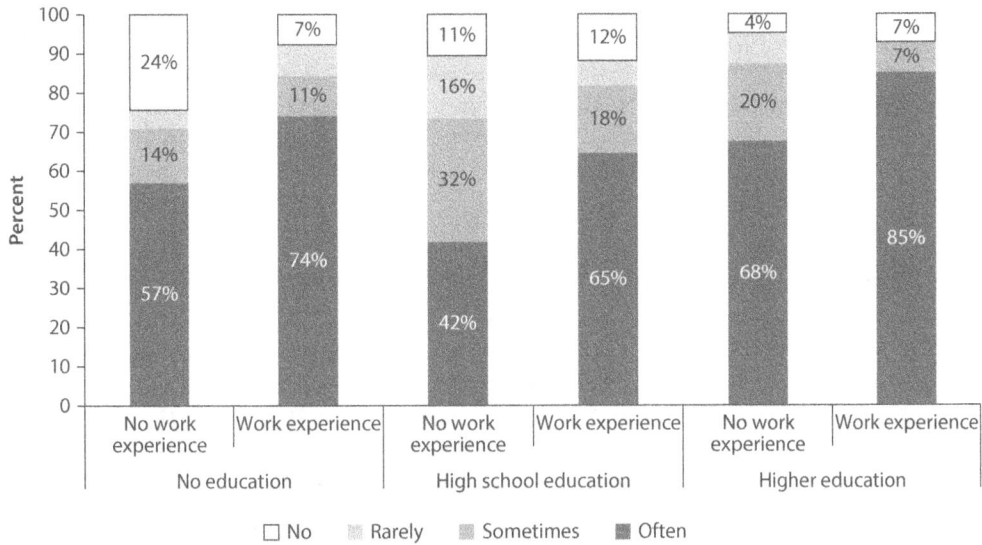

Source: World Bank, 2012, Libya Rapid Labor Market Assessment, Washington, DC.

Figure 5.9 Skills Most in Demand versus Most Difficult to Recruit

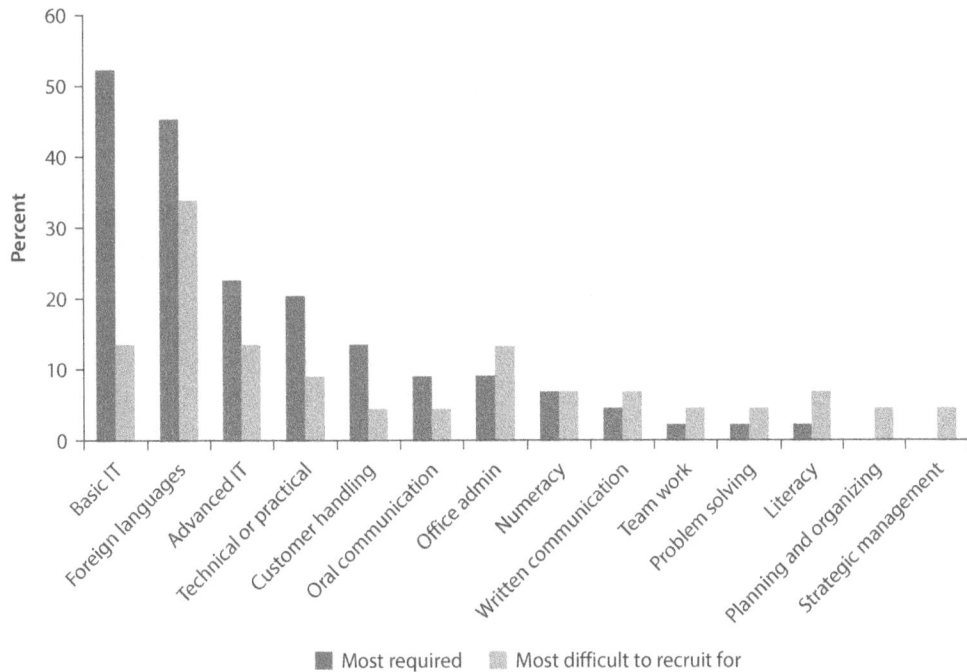

Source: World Bank, 2012, Libya Rapid Labor Market Assessment, Washington, DC.
Note: IT = information technology.

job training, 12 percent offer English language courses, and 37 percent send their staff abroad for training.[6] Thirty-five percent offer certified or formal training for industrial, engineering, or software qualifications.[7] Of these firms, 53 percent provide certified training in-house and 35 percent through Libya-based external training providers,[8] with the remainder (12 percent) sending staff abroad for certified training. Firms indicated that most training is procured from a variety of relatively small providers.

Due to existing labor laws, internships may be serving as a means to hire temporary workers for menial tasks rather than providing adequate job training. For example, many hotels may offer large numbers of cleaning and waiting "internships" to young Libyans during busy periods. One firm appeared to have the most formalized internship scheme, in which 10 people per year are offered the opportunity to gain experience in a variety of roles (production technician, administration, maintenance engineer, or professional). Another firm offered an apprenticeship for new carpenters. Some construction and engineering firms offer more technical opportunities for young engineers.

Rather than a willingness to pay, the main barrier to training at firms is a lack of required training providers. Overall, with the exception of a few highly specialized software training programs, firms were rarely impressed with external training providers, giving an average performance rating of 60 percent. One firm has its own training center and also uses an external private training provider based abroad for management and specialist distribution training. Eighty percent of firms that do not provide formal training would do so if training providers were available. Forty percent indicate that they require technical support on guiding and developing training policies and programs. Only 12 percent of firms indicated that funding was a barrier to training workers.

Labor Regulations

Most firms support reforming labor policy regarding foreign labor, social protection, and contracts. Only 56 percent of firms' representatives were familiar with Libya's labor code, *Law Number 12 of 2010 Concerning Labor Relations* (figure 5.10). Fifteen percent of firms familiar with the labor code advocate for reforms to facilitate hiring foreign workers, particularly highly skilled workers. Ten percent also support better social protection and rights for workers, particularly for training benefits, working hours, and wages. Six percent advocate for easier contracting procedures, given their relative complexity and high administrative costs. Six percent of firms aim to improve employers' rights, notably regarding ease of firing under-performing or persistently absent workers. Other firms indicated that they did not understand certain articles of the labor code regarding entitlements, such as paid vacation and sick leave policies (Articles 30 and 33, respectively).

Labor legislation pertaining to foreign workers is unclear to most firms. While 77 percent of firms employ foreign workers, only 28 percent understand the

Figure 5.10   Libyan Firms Advocating for Labor Code Reforms by Type of Reform

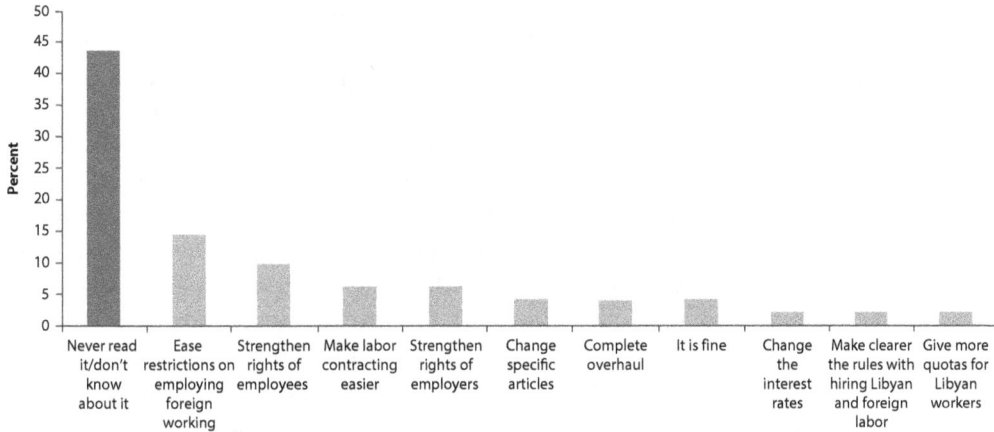

Source: World Bank, 2012, Libya Rapid Labor Market Assessment, Washington, DC.

regulations for employing foreign labor. The quota for Libyan nationals is officially 25 percent under Article 51, yet is interpreted broadly by firms in the private and public sectors. Among the private sector, most firms report a minimum quota of 33 percent Libyan nationals is required. Among the public sector, the hiring rules claimed by firms range from 20 percent to 85 percent Libyan nationals. Hiring foreign workers is more regulated in the public sector. Overall, 30 percent felt that it was often difficult to meet the official quota of 25 percent.

Conclusions

In the short term, employment growth in Libya likely may come from small and medium enterprises, until economic diversification occurs and public sector employment is reformed. In the near term, reforms will be needed to create private sector jobs, namely by (a) jump-starting economic diversification, (b) creating a competitively skilled labor force, and (c) improving the design of social protection systems and labor regulations. In parallel, an immediate careful assessment of public sector employment is needed to prepare a strategy for gradual reform in the short to medium term. This two-pronged, sequential approach will help to transform the labor market to improve its outcomes and foster sustainable growth for a stable, productive workforce. To refine the reform program, an in-depth assessment of the labor market should follow, focusing on the landscape and political economy of labor market institutions in Libya, preferences and skills of job seekers, and underlying factors influencing job creation from the perspective of employers.

Overall, firms perceived that their business cycles were resuming following interruptions in production during the conflict, and were positive about short- and long-term growth. This optimism was the case in every sector except for construction, which was seen to be largely unrecovered due to the halting of many large government projects. The six economic sectors that represent the majority of the employment opportunities in the private sector are construction, hospitality, trade, agriculture, services, and manufacturing. Many firms reported recruiting Libyan staff while hiring a small number of qualified and unqualified foreign workers to fulfill job needs that remained. Some firms had replaced foreign labor with Libyan labor following the revolution.

Nevertheless, the current size of the private sector hardly can be expected to automatically generate the number of jobs needed to tackle Libya's unemployment. While managers expected a growth of approximately 6 percent in each of the coming two years, the impact of this growth on employment levels of Libyans was expected to be fairly small, because many firms expected to fill their positions with foreign labor. Notably, many firms expressed a willingness to pay for training, an opportunity that should be seized to directly meet their labor force skills development needs. Reforms are needed to improve the business climate, policy regarding labor and social benefits, and skills development and active labor market programs.

Notes

1. Interview with Tripoli City Council Economic Section, May 2012.
2. Oxford Business Group, *The Report Libya 2010*. United Kingdom (2010), 216.
3. World Bank, *Libya Investment Climate* (Washington, DC: World Bank, 2011), 10.
4. World Bank, *Libya Investment Climate*.
5. Approximately 37 private firms and 6 public firms offer financial and nonfinancial benefits to workers. Large private firms and virtually all SOEs offer health insurance. Some firms reported offering benefits packages that include monthly wage increases, firm cars, and laptops. Small firms are much less likely to offer benefits, but some offer smaller benefits such as language courses, mobile phone credit, or extra paid vacation for certain occasions (weddings).
6. Firms sending employees abroad for training included a dairy manufacturing firm (for training on factory equipment at manufacturers' premises), a construction firm (using an engineering center abroad), and a firm sending staff to a sister site abroad for in-house training.
7. Fifty percent of the firms give recognized qualifications, such as the "International Computer Driving License" or specific industrial safety qualifications. The other 50 percent offer on-demand training for specialized engineering or database software. Eight percent (three firms) routinely offer formal training, including one firm that has implemented a rigorous internal training scheme with monthly reports and two firms in the construction sector that have formal training schemes for IT literacy and accounting software.
8. A wide range of Libyan training providers are used for various training programs, including Microsoft-certified management and administrative training centers. The hospitality industry uses specialized training centers, including the publicly managed hospitality training center in Tripoli, the Al-Amia Center in Benghazi, and the Egypt-Malaysia Hospitality Training Centre in Tripoli.

CHAPTER 6

Policy Implications: Emerging Opportunities during Transition

Summary of Findings and Key Challenges

Although political instability remains the most significant barrier to jobs and reintegration in Libya, labor market trends also reflect structural challenges. At the same time, emerging job opportunities for youth and combatants can play an important role in stabilization and state-building. Key employment challenges and areas for reform include:

- **Business climate impeding labor demand**: Inadequate access to finance and business regulations reduce incentives for firms to invest, particularly in emerging sectors such as infrastructure, trade, services, and agribusiness[1]
- **Public sector as employer of choice**: Dominance of the public sector and state-owned enterprises in the economy
- **Labor regulations**: Structure of employment contracts, quotas for nationals and non-nationals, training requirements, and hiring and firing policies, among others
- **Dichotomy of social security policies between the public and private sectors**: Low social insurance coverage in the private sector and queuing for public sector jobs
- **Job-relevant skills**: Challenges faced by firms in recruiting qualified Libyans for both highly and low-skilled jobs and the need to reskill ex-combatants for jobs outside the security sector
- **School-to-work transition**: Weak labor market insertion among youth and women and one of the world's highest unemployment rates among university graduates.

Libya's labor market challenges reflect three types of issues: fundamental obstacles, labor-policy-related barriers, and priority issues specific to its current context. Challenges related to governance, institutions, and the business climate

Figure 6.1 Policy Pathway to Jobs and Reintegration for Libya

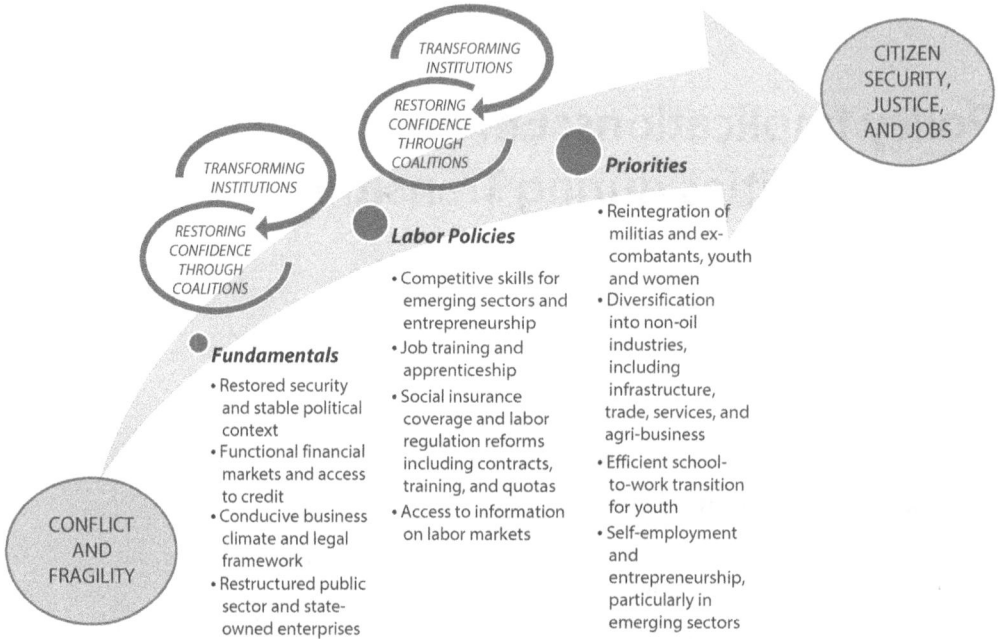

Source: World Bank staff.

remain the primary barriers to catalyze private-sector-led growth. The way that Libya's regulations, training, and social security policies are designed also may impede, rather than create, incentives to diversify the economy. In addition, specific policies and programs may be needed to accelerate reintegration for ex-combatants and jobs for youth and women, including self-employment in new sectors. To address these challenges, a comprehensive jobs strategy should be developed to launch a multifaceted program of reforms and interventions in the short to long term, discussed in the next section (figure 6.1).

Framework for a Comprehensive Jobs Strategy

A comprehensive jobs strategy should include short-term measures for Libya's stabilization that can pave the way for long-term job creation and diversification. The experiences of other middle-income countries in East Asia and Pacific, Latin America, Eastern Europe, and South Asia shed light on options for employment and reintegration in fragile contexts. For example, the resilience and accelerated pace of growth in East Asia and Pacific highlights the role of strong private-sector-led economic diversification coupled with high levels of human capital (box 6.1). The rest of this section does not prescribe a specific jobs strategy but rather lays out key areas for consideration toward developing such a strategy. Key policy objectives include (a) building the fundamentals for sustainable, diversified growth to restore security and stable institutions, a well-functioning financial

---

Box 6.1 Weathering Crises through Work in East Asia and Pacific

Whether conflict, political fragility, or financial crises, the experience of the East Asia and Pacific Region highlights how work has helped to build resilience. Countries including China, Indonesia, the Republic of Korea, Thailand, and Vietnam have experienced growth and economic diversification at historically unprecedented rates for several reasons.

Sound macrofiscal policies, deeper global integration, and economic institutions in the East Asia and Pacific Region have accelerated private-sector-led growth, stimulated demand for work, and enhanced resilience during crises such as the financial crisis of 2008–10 unlike few other regions in the world. Price stability, low public debt, and relatively light taxation have encouraged business and investment.

Widespread access to adequate health and an increasingly competitive educational system have ensured a strong foundation of human capital. Labor productivity has risen higher elsewhere. Since 2000, China has experienced a three-fold increase and Vietnam a two-fold increase.

Although many challenges remain, social insurance policies and labor regulations, such as minimum wage, employment protection legislation, and activation policies, have helped stimulate formal work. Given its speed of structural transformation, an evolving skills profile, and increasing integration with the global economy, the East Asia and Pacific Region has been able to sustain high growth rates and job creation through crises.

Source: Adapted from World Bank, 2014, East Asia and Pacific at Work: Employment, Enterprise, and Well-Being, Washington, DC.

---

market, and a competitive investment climate over the long run; and (b) improving the efficiency of labor market insertion programs for youth in the short run, prioritizing militias and ex-combatants. Policy recommendations follow for the fundamentals, labor policies, and priorities toward reaching these objectives (table 6.1).

Fundamentals: Restoring Security for a Competitive Business Climate

One of the most fundamental constraints facing Libya is the dominance of the public sector in the economy from production to service delivery, crowding out the private sector. Creating a vibrant business climate for the private sector is critical to establish a maturely functioning financial market, which is relatively absent in Libya. A new regulatory framework for investment and labor policies is recommended to strengthen Libya's competitive potential, building on lessons learned from other oil- and resource-rich countries that have diversified their economies.

Promoting employment in the private sector will mean a shift in civil service employment and potential restructuring of state-owned enterprises. An evaluation of civil service employment is needed to assess remuneration policies, to what extent performance is rewarded, and qualifications and criteria for hiring.

Table 6.1   Summary of Policy Recommendations for Libya

Policy recommendations	Time horizon
Fundamentals	
Private sector growth	
Expand business services to firms with a focus on emerging sectors	Short-term
Transform role of chambers of commerce to enhance innovation, entrepreneurship training, and job placement	Short-term
Strengthen the financial market, expand access to credit, and simplify regulation	Mid-term
Develop new framework for business regulations and governance to expand incentives for growth in emerging sectors	Mid-term
Public sector restructuring	
Reform civil service employment regulations	Mid-long term
Restructure public services and state-owned enterprises	Long-term
Labor policies	
Job training and active labor market programs	
Develop public-private apprenticeships and on-the-job training	Short-term
Develop regional and global partnerships for certified skills development programs and introduce performance-based contracting for institutional training	Short-term
Job matching	
Strategically orient career and job coaching services	Short-term
Stimulate and mobilize private intermediation design, standardization, certification, and financing mechanisms	Mid-term
Access to labor market information	
Improve quality and availability of labor market data, evaluation, and information systems, including labor demand forecasting, skills, wages and benefits, and migration	Short-term
Social insurance and labor regulations	
Reform labor regulations regarding recruitment, wages, benefits and working conditions (contract law), migration policies	Mid-term
Strengthen social security coverage, sustainability, and incentives, particularly for private sector and informal workers	Mid-term
Educational reforms	
Introduce pre-graduate skills development and on-the-job training	Long-term
Restructure vocational education for demand-driven training and expand certified skills development programs	Long-term
Adapt basic and higher education to economic development strategy	Long-term
Priorities	
Establish short-term job training and public service programs for ex-combatants and youth through public-private partnerships (PPPs)	Short-term
Integrate monitoring of ex-combatants by merging WAC and MOL job seeker databases	Short-term
Facilitate access to credit and foreign investment in emerging, target sectors, among them tourism, agri-business, manufacturing, education, and health	Mid-term

Source: World Bank staff.
Note: WAC = Warriors Affairs Commission; MOL = Ministry of Labor.

The potential role of the private sector in public-private partnerships (PPPs) can take on various levels and types of co-financing, co-management, and/or co-delivery of services and stakes in state-owned enterprises (SOEs). These options will need to be examined from the perspective of employment generation. Depending on the type of reforms needed, it will be important to ensure that adequate support to workers is given: temporary income support, retraining, or other forms of social protection during transition.

Labor Policies: Reorienting Regulations and Skills for Good Jobs

Libya's current labor regulations and social security policies may be impeding, not facilitating, job creation. In 2012 Libya initiated a review of its labor code and the development of a new law to enable unions to form and engage in social dialogue. This assessment did not include an in-depth evaluation of these issues but has identified some areas for further analysis. The quota system for nationals, social benefits, and the way that contracts are structured are policies that, depending on how they are reformed, can either repel or attract investors. There also is a need to examine how to gradually enhance social security coverage while promoting private sector investment. Finally, labor migration policies need to be reviewed to ensure that Libya has the right labor force skills while ensuring adequate social protection for workers.

The labor force also may not be meeting the skills demands of the labor market due to the mismatch of quality and relevance between education and active labor market programs. An evaluation of Libya's basic, higher, and vocational educational system was outside the scope of this assessment. However, the analysis revealed both high unemployment among university graduates and problems reported by firms in recruiting semiskilled workers. Libya has not participated in international basic education competency tests, and little information is available on the quality of education. Therefore, there is a need to evaluate Libya's educational system and reforms that might be needed in the short to long term to better equip graduates at all levels with the skills needed by the labor market.

Short-term interventions may not necessarily create new jobs but can facilitate job placement, particularly for semiskilled and highly skilled job seekers who can be retrained. The 2012 Bank assessment identified seven potential categories of job seekers, including more active job seekers willing to accept less highly skilled jobs and those willing to be retrained. This group collectively represents 30 percent to 56 percent of the unemployed. Building job-relevant skills and retraining for youth and women targeted at firms' demands improve prospects for both wage employment and entrepreneurship. Improving their prospects is especially the case for ex-combatants who have lost these skills over time, as shown in the case of reintegration efforts throughout parts of South Asia.[2]

Apprenticeship and on-the-job training and skills certification may accelerate job insertion in Libya, particularly when tailored to pre-identified jobs and providers' performance is rewarded. A range of approaches exist to design these programs to directly meet the demands of hiring firms, including tying skills development to pre-identified jobs (appendix C). The experience of Mexico (box 6.2) and Bosnia and Herzegovina (box 6.3) highlight the strong impact that on-the-job training can have on employment and earnings, including for ex-combatants in the case of Bosnia and Herzegovina. Innovative collaboration between the public and private sectors and civil society is taking root in Libya for job placement and training services. This collaboration can be expanded to other programs (box 6.4).

Box 6.2   Effects of Job Training and Placement in Mexico

While various approaches to skills development, job search, and subsidy schemes can improve employment outcomes, **on-the-job (OTJ) training** may be particularly relevant to Libya's context. For example, evidence from impact evaluations conducted in Mexico and Bosnia and Herzegovina show the positive impact that OTJ has had on employment and income, especially when targeted well and combined with other interventions.[a]

Faced with poor macroeconomic conditions, high informality, and rampant youth unemployment, in 1984 **Mexico** launched the *Programa de Becas de Capacitación para Trabajadores Desempleados* (PROBECAT) program, later changed to *Becat*. The program consisted of three-month paid training to jobseekers, initially at vocational training centers and eventually OTJ at firms. The program anticipated that, following the OTJ, most workers would be hired through the firm and the remainder supported by job placement services under the scheme. The biggest benefits on employment, particularly salaried employment, generally have come from the OTJ program.[b] The effects were greatest for women, those with secondary schooling or above, and those who first took school-based training. The PROBECAT program has had smaller effects on entrepreneurship.

Source: World Bank staff.
a. Independent Evaluation Group, *World Bank and IFC Support for Youth Employment Programs* (Washington, DC: World Bank, 2013).
b. M. Delajara, S. Freije, and I. Soloaga, "An Evaluation of Training for the Unemployed in Mexico." Working Paper OVE/WP-09/06, Inter-American Development Bank (IADB), Office of Evaluation and Oversight, Washington, DC (2006).

Box 6.3   Jobs and Reintegration in Bosnia and Herzegovina

Similar to the Mexico's experience, OTJ, combined with job search assistance and improved labor market information availability, has helped reintegrate ex-combatants in **Bosnia and Herzegovina**. From 1996–99, the Emergency Demobilization and Reintegration Program financed primarily OTJ at local firms (86 percent of the contracts to training providers) as well as institution-based training (7 percent of contracts) and job counseling (7 percent of

box continues next page

Box 6.3 Jobs and Reintegration in Bosnia and Herzegovina *(continued)*

contracts) through competitive, performance-based contracts. Approximately 300,000 demobilized soldiers benefited from the program. Incentives were introduced to reward performance based on job placement rates. To ensure the relevance of the training and job placement, providers had to commit to hire 80 percent of the people they had trained.

An evaluation showed that six months after completion of the program, employment and wages significantly increased regardless of age, gender, or educational level.[3] Similar to the Mexican experience, the strength of these interventions lies in their ability to target job training at the needs of the private sector.

Source: World Bank staff.

Box 6.4 Local Public-Private Partnerships in Libya

In the midst of Libya's transition, innovative public-private partnerships for job promotion have emerged at the local level. In April 2014, the Tripoli Local Council, the largest of Libya's three main municipal seats, and the Tawakkel Libya Foundation for Development, a nongovernmental organization (NGO) facilitating job seeker-private sector networking and entrepreneurship, opened their doors to a new employment center housed at the municipality's office. The center benefits from financial and in-kind support from the municipality, including generous office and conferencing space on its premises and a small team of full-time staff.

Services include a range of job placement support services: (a) organizing job fairs, workshops, and individual training sessions to assist with the job search and interviewing process; (b) providing intermediation services between job seekers and employment opportunities through creating a network of firms and entrepreneurship opportunities; (c) developing relationships with networks of employers and services to assist in identifying and hiring staff; and (d) mobilizing and sharing information with jobseekers on firm profiles, wages, and entrepreneurship opportunities.

The center is developing performance targets and mechanisms to monitor beneficiaries' perceptions of its services, both job seekers and potential employers. Indicators planned include job placement rates for job seekers, employment rates for university graduates, and performance ratings by beneficiaries and employers of employment services. This PPP initiative is the first in Libya to bring together public financing with the private sector to facilitate employment.

Moving forward, the center serves as an example to public-private partnerships for the delivery of labor programs. Scale-up can be achieved by coordinating with the Ministry of Labor (MOL) and Warriors Affairs Commission (WAC) databases and public employment centers to improve matching and job training linked directly with pre-identified profiles, skills, and needs from the private sector.

Source: World Bank staff.

Improving the relevance of vocational education can help to develop new sectors and entrepreneurship in Libya. When tied to entrepreneurship training, vocational training also can fill untapped potential for self-employment. While not all job seekers are qualified to become successful entrepreneurs, targeting key sectors and sufficient reconversion training can lead to gainful employment opportunities.

Improving the quality of, and access to, labor market information will enable better design of labor policies. Evidence on skills, competencies, earnings and benefits, and the demand for labor is needed through regular surveys and the development of administrative systems for collecting data and statistics. As Libya begins to innovate and reform labor market programs, monitoring and evaluating these programs will help to determine which interventions are most effective. Creating a consolidated database and information system also will facilitate access to information for employers and jobseekers alike.

Priorities: Reintegration and Emerging Sectors

Specific policies can be designed to integrate youth, ex-combatants, and women into the labor market, particularly in emerging sectors. Support to ex-combatant economic integration has been shown to be a crucial element of the state-building process and helps them channel their skills into productive futures. On-the-job training and apprenticeship programs would improve the employability of job seekers, in addition to other training and public service programs that can be effective for low-skilled workers. To help promote the growth of firms, entrepreneurship training for qualified candidates can be developed in partnership with Libya's business associations and chambers of commerce.

Conclusions

As Libya's transition unfolds, building coalitions to improve the employment outlook will help support long-term state-building. On one hand, Libya's challenges are similar to those faced by the rest of Middle East and North Africa, as well as by other middle-income and fragile contexts. On the other hand, Libya needs to both fill a long-standing, deep institutional vacuum *and* facilitate reconciliation among rival factions in a nascent state. Significant structural and institutional reforms are needed.

Coalition-building can accelerate the pace of change. Innovative public-private collaboration is emerging in Libya. These partnerships can accelerate jobs and reintegration, particularly for untapped, new sectors such as trade, services, tourism, and agribusiness. Going forward, the development of a jobs strategy for the short to long term that is based on Libya's economic vision is needed. It will need to address the range of challenges to Libya's business climate, labor market institutions, and educational system. Such a strategy will help to secure a stable future for Libya.

Notes

1. A detailed discussion of private sector development issues is outside the scope of this report.
2. World Bank, "Creating Jobs in Conflict-Affected Areas," in *More and Better Jobs in South Asia* (Washington, DC: World Bank, 2012).
3. J. Benus, J. Rude, and S Patrabansh, "Impact of the Emergency Demobilization and Reintegration Project in Bosnia and Herzegovina," Department of Labor, Bureau of International Affairs, Development Impact Evaluation (DIME), and U.S. Agency for International Development (USAID), Washington, DC (2001).

Rapid Labor Market Assessment Methodology

Objectives

The overall objective of the 2012 Rapid Labor Market Assessment was to rapidly determine the profiles, needs, and preferences of the labor market and job insertion programs from the perspectives of a small sample of job seekers and employers. The specific objectives were to:

- Assess the gap between the skills demanded by different economic sectors and firm typologies, and the skills available in the Libyan population segments and population typologies
- Identify institutions that support the labor market or are involved in matching supply with demand such as job seeker centers, public and private training centers, business associations, and chambers of commerce
- Conduct a rapid assessment of the linkages and roles of these institutions in the labor market toward operationalizing the labor market entry strategies or labor absorption strategies outlined above
- Briefly test the validity of existing supply and demand databases, for example, how representative are the existing job seeker and firm databases held by different Libyan government institutions.

Regarding labor supply, the objectives were to:

- Develop detailed case studies that describe the labor supply characteristics of different population segments and population typologies, including information on demographic profiles; current perspectives on employment preferences and goals; levels of education, skill, and work experience; positions in and understanding of the labor market
- Outline options for labor market entry strategies for each population segment and population typology

- Develop preliminary answers to unanswered questions regarding the Libyan labor supply, such as the willingness to work in different types of jobs, in the public versus private sector, and regarding the perspectives of former combatants' willingness to work
- Where possible, provide estimates of sizes of population segments and population typologies.

Regarding labor demand, the objectives were to:

- Develop detailed case studies for a range of economic sectors that describe the labor demand characteristics, including business development perspectives; employment profiles; and skills demand in small, medium, and large firms
- Outline shorter and longer term labor absorption strategies for each economic sector and firm typology
- Develop preliminary answers to unanswered questions regarding Libyan labor demand, such as firms' hiring practices of Libyan and foreign workforce, willingness to invest in training, and preference for in-house (firm-based) or external training
- Provide estimates of the short- and long-term labor demand, disaggregated by skill set and sectors where possible
- Propose a typology to map low-to-high potential sectors for employment creation based on a proposed set of clear criteria and characteristics.

Labor Supply Assessment

In-depth interviews (IDIs) were conducted with 10 population segments identified according to a combination of characteristics including age, gender, education level, and employment status (table A.1). To reflect Libya's "youth bulge," 6 of the 10 population segments were youth focused. These segments included equal numbers of male and female respondents, and were disaggregated into two main employment characteristics (gainfully employed or un/under-employed) and a range of education levels (degree-level, high school or vocational, and uneducated). The next two segments focused on un/under-employed middle-aged individuals to understand their situations in the labor market. The final two population segments were current, occasional, and former (ex)combatants (males only); and civil servants who had been pushed out of the civil service due to political disagreements after the conflict. The latter group was reluctant to participate in interviews.

For this research, "youth" are 15–25 years of age and middle-aged people are 26–40 years of age. Table A.1 shows the justification for selecting each population segment and the numbers of interviews conducted in each.

By design, a majority of the interviews were conducted in the three main labor markets: Tripoli, Benghazi, and Misratah (table A.2). The research team also

Table A.1 Population Groups Included in Rapid Assessment

Population group		Justification	Sample size (n)
1	Gainfully employed degree-educated male and female youth	To assess mechanisms for successful labor market entry for well-educated youth	9 (6)
2	Gainfully employed vocationally trained or secondary-school-educated male or female youth	To assess mechanisms for successful labor market entry for vocationally and mid-level-educated youth	7 (6)
3	Gainfully employed uneducated (primary school only) male and female youth	To assess mechanisms for successful labor market entry for uneducated youth	6 (6)
4	Un- or under-employed degree-educated male and female youth	To assess situations, barriers, and motivations for labor market entry for well-educated but un- or under-employed youth	6 (6)
5	Un- or under-employed vocationally trained or secondary-school-educated male and female youth	To assess situations, barriers, and motivations for labor market entry for vocationally and mid-level educated youth	8 (6)
6	Un- or under-employed uneducated (primary school only) male and female youth	To assess situations, barriers, and motivations for labor market entry for youth with very low education levels	6 (6)
7	Un- or under-employed degree-educated male and female middle-aged Libyans	To assess situations, barriers, and motivations for labor market entry for well-educated but un- or under-employed middle-aged Libyans	7 (6)
8	Un- or under-employed vocationally trained or secondary-school-educated male and female middle-aged Libyans	To assess situations, barriers, and motivations for labor market entry for vocationally and mid-level educated but un- or under-employed middle-aged Libyans	7 (6)
9	Current and occasional irregular combatants (all ages)	To assess situations, barriers, and motivations for labor market (re-) entry for people using arms outside of security institutions	11 (6)
10	Recently disengaged civil servants, particularly police (all ages)*	To assess situations, barriers, and motivations for labor market (re-) entry for disengaged civil servants	0 (6)
		Total In-Depth Interviews	**67 (60)**

Source: World Bank staff.

travelled to Zuwara, Qarabuli, and Ajdabiyah to gain a rapid understanding of the labor market in these smaller population centers. The south of the country was not visited due to the short duration of the project. The research team employed a number of women to conduct the interviews. As a result, a total of 22 women were interviewed (32 percent), a fair achievement considering some of the rather difficult research locations and the cultural sensitivities with interviewing women. Table A.2 shows the location breakdown of the interviews.

Labor Demand Assessment

Six economic sectors of interest were selected according to a two-stage filter that qualitatively examined short- and long-term employment potential in each sector (table A.3). The sectors were construction, manufacturing, trade,

Table A.2 Research Locations and Gender Balance

		Tripoli	Misratah	Benghazi	Qarabuli	Ajdabiyah	Zuwara	Total
1	Gainfully employed degree-educated male and female youth	M	0	1	1	0	0	1	**3**
		F	2	3	1	0	0	0	**6**
2	Gainfully employed vocationally trained or secondary-school-educated male or female youth	M	1	1	1	1	1	0	**5**
		F	0	0	1	0	0	1	**2**
3	Gainfully employed uneducated (primary school only) male and female youth	M	1	1	1	1	0	0	**4**
		F	1	0	1	0	0	0	**2**
4	Un- or under-employed degree-educated male and female youth	M	2	1	0	0	0	1	**4**
		F	1	0	1	0	0		**2**
5	Un- or under-employed vocationally trained or secondary-school-educated male and female youth	M	2	1	1	0	1	1	**6**
		F	1	0	1	0	0	0	**2**
6	Un- or under-employed uneducated (primary school only) male and female youth	M	1	1	1	1	0	0	**4**
		F	1	0	1	0	0	0	**2**
7	Un- or under-employed degree-educated male and female middle-aged Libyans	M	0	1	1	1	1	0	**4**
		F	2	0	1	0	0	0	**3**
8	Un- or under-employed vocationally trained or secondary-school-educated male and female middle-aged Libyans	M	0	2	1	0	1	0	**4**
		F	1	1	1	0	0	0	**3**
9	Current and occasional irregular combatants (all ages)	M	2	1	4	1	1	2	**11**
	Total		**18**	**14**	**19**	**5**	**5**	**6**	**67**

Source: World Bank.

agriculture/fisheries, hospitality, and services. Thus, firms in economic sectors that are not believed to hold promise for short-term employment opportunities will not be considered for research in this project. Within each segment, approximately 10 firms were interviewed according to variables including:

- **Firm size**—Small, medium, or large
- **Ownership**—Public or private
- **Location**—Tripoli, Benghazi, or Misratah.

Firms were selected using literature reviews, the Investment Climate Assessment (ICA) 2010 database, Key Informant Interviews (KIIs), Privatization and Investment Board (PIB) databases, and direct research (for smaller firms). A total of 61 firms were interviewed (table A.3).

Table A.3 Interviewed Firms and Locations

1. CONSTRUCTION

		Tripoli	Benghazi	Misrata	
PRIVATE	Small	2 Al Manarah, Panorama Libya			
	Medium	1 Al Mutaheda	1 Libya Construction Technology Company (LCTC)	2 Qasr Al Kajalil, Jiim Company	
	Large				
PUBLIC	Medium				
	Large	3 LIDCO, The Engineering Consultancy, Al Inma for Real Estate	1 Company of Public Works		
	TOTAL	6	2	2	10

2. MANUFACTURING

		Tripoli	Benghazi	Misrata	
PRIVATE	Small	2 Bustan (soap) and Najma (soup)	1 Al Zahraa (paperbags)		
	Medium	1 Al Hajaji (carpentry)			
	Large	2 Africa Company (soft drinks/pepsi), Jifara (food)	1 Libyan Cement Company (LCC)	1 Al Naseem (dairy)	
PUBLIC	Medium				
	Large	2 Al Moukhtar (various), Tobacco Factory (cigarettes)			
	TOTAL	7	2	1	10

3. TRADE

		Tripoli	Benghazi	Misrata	
PRIVATE	Small	1 Al Manzel Al Raki		2 Taqadoum Al Hadeeth, Tawareg Company	
	Medium	1 Jawharit Africa		1 Tasheid Company	
	Large	1 Al Rayaheen			
PUBLIC	Medium		2 HB Group, Al Hawari		
	Large				
	TOTAL	3	2	3	8

table continues next page

Table A.3 Interviewed Firms and Locations (continued)

4. AGRICULTURE & FISHING

		Tripoli	Benghazi	Misrata
PRIVATE	Small	3 Al Hashmi Farm & Amar Farm & Ibna Alaji Co.		2 Al Baher Al Hadeer
	Medium	2 Blue Sea Fishing & Younes Al Maharji Farms		
	Large			
PUBLIC	Medium			
	Large			1 The Agriculture Company
	TOTAL	5	0	3
				8

5. HOTELS & RESTAURANTS

		Tripoli	Benghazi	Misrata
PRIVATE	Small	4 Al Baaja Café, Al Kadeema Co, Al Garaa Pizza, Dekna Hotel		1 Al Kabeer Hotel
	Medium	2 Al Massa Hotel and Waddan Hotel	2 Nouran Hotel, Pizza Restaurant	1 Al Baraka Hotel
	Large			
PUBLIC	Medium			
	Large	2 Bab Al Baher & Hotel Al Kabeer	1 Tibesty Hotel	
	TOTAL	8	3	2
				13

6. SERVICES & COMMS

		Tripoli	Benghazi	Misrata
PRIVATE	Small	4 Intaj Media, Burj advertising, Hedaa Dhahaby (shoe repair), Al Aali	1 Mina Agency	2 Teika (tire repair), Al Hares Security
	Medium	2 Istishari Computer Repair, Al Mutahidoon Legal Advisors		
	Large			
PUBLIC	Medium			
	Large	2 LTT, Al Medina Multimedia		1 Misrata Free Zone Company
	TOTAL	8	1	3
				12
	GRAND TOTAL	**37**	**10**	**14**
				61

Source: World Bank staff.
Note: LIDCO = Libyan Investment and Development Firm.

Detailed questionnaires of 90 questions and 70 questions were developed for the supply- (job seekers) and demand-side (firms) interviews, respectively. They are explained and shown in appendix B.

Challenges

It is worth noting the challenges faced conducting the research. At the macro level, obtaining information from the senior levels of the Ministries of Planning and Labor was difficult. Officials at lower levels often were helpfully frank in their opinions of the information and processes they with which they were involved. Officials at the Statistics Bureau were very accommodating.

For the supply assessment, difficulties were encountered in engaging female respondents. Throughout the research an effort was made to train and employ female interviewers in each location.

For the demand side, gaining access to government firms was extremely difficult because an air of suspicion of researchers prevailed. Multiple visits and approval letters nearly always were required before the interviewers could access the relevant managers. Most managers struggled to differentiate between all the skills-based questions. The long interviews often meant that interviewers struggled to maintain the attention of the managers. Future assessments can refine the methodology to address these challenges.

Rapid Labor Market Assessment Questionnaire Design

Both the supply- and demand-side questionnaires were translated into Arabic and administered face-to-face.

For the supply-side research, a 90-question questionnaire was developed in coordination with the World Bank to cover all population segments. The questionnaire included additional blocks of questions to cover active and occasional combatant and civil servants. The questionnaire was structure as a quantitative instrument to collect data and allow for the development of case studies (table B.1).

Table B.1   Structure of Supply-Side (Job-seekers') Questionnaire

Question block		Intended research outcome
A	Interview details	
B	Demographic profile	
C	Employment profile	Details about current primary and secondary jobs
D	Work history	Is lack of experience a barrier to find a job? How long does it take for various profiles to find a job?
E	Support network	Is the lack of a support network a barrier to find a job? Conversely, is a strong network limiting motivation?
F	Motivation	What are Libyans of various profiles ready to do as jobs?
G	Knowledge of labor market	Where do Libyans get information about jobs? How are their expectations matched with their profiles?
H	Skills	Self-assessment of skills/lack thereof, skills most used in previous jobs and work experience, specific training in certain skills, most valued skills, most desired skills
I	Needs	Individual needs and suggestions for how the government can make it easier to find a job
J	Women in the workplace	Barriers to finding jobs, most and least rewarding jobs for women
K	Perspectives	Outlook on short- and long-term future
L	Displaced civil servants	Specific issues linked to civil servants who lost their positions during the revolution
M	Combatants/ex-combatants	Specific issues linked to combat

Source: World Bank staff.

For the demand-side research, a 70-question questionnaire was developed for all firms, regardless of size, industry, or formality (table B.2). To support building comparable case studies, the questionnaires will be largely quantitative but also include open questions to cope with the wide variation in business situations.

Table B.2 Structure of Demand-Side (Firms') Questionnaire

Question block		Intended research outcome
A	Interview details	
B	Firm profile	
C	Current employees	Main employment statistics and recent variations
D	Turnover/retention	Evaluate the volatility of Libyan labor market by sector. What keeps Libyans in the same firm?
E	Skills	What are the most important skills required in the short-term for Libyan workers to have?
F	Training/apprenticeship	Are firms involved in capacity building? What is their willingness to pay for or invest in training, either in-house, or externally?
G	Recruitment methods	What are the most common/efficient recruitment methods for various categories of employees?
H	Perspective of growth	What sectors will recruit in the near future?
I	Institutions	How useful is the institutional fabric around firms, notably on promoting employment? Are organizations legally bound to employ and train Libyans, and do they follow the law?

Source: World Bank staff.

Operational Framework for a Public-Private Job Training and Placement System

Figure C.1 Public-Private Job Training and Placement Framework

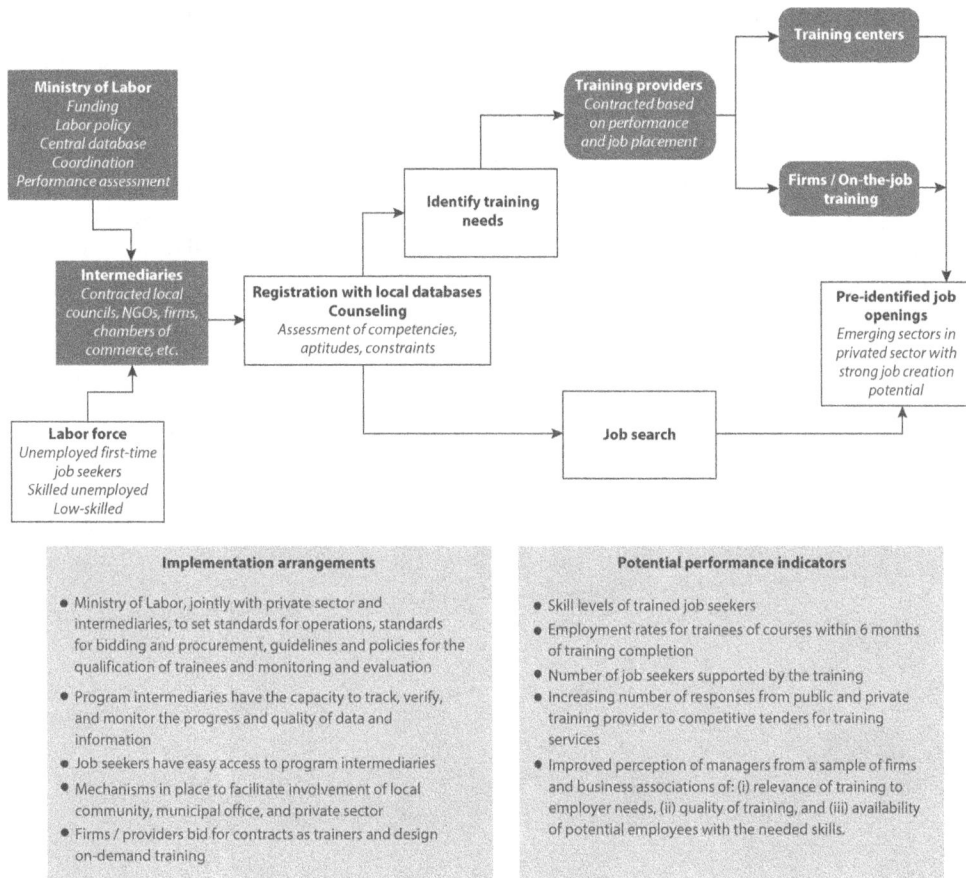

Implementation arrangements

- Ministry of Labor, jointly with private sector and intermediaries, to set standards for operations, standards for bidding and procurement, guidelines and policies for the qualification of trainees and monitoring and evaluation
- Program intermediaries have the capacity to track, verify, and monitor the progress and quality of data and information
- Job seekers have easy access to program intermediaries
- Mechanisms in place to facilitate involvement of local community, municipal office, and private sector
- Firms / providers bid for contracts as trainers and design on-demand training

Potential performance indicators

- Skill levels of trained job seekers
- Employment rates for trainees of courses within 6 months of training completion
- Number of job seekers supported by the training
- Increasing number of responses from public and private training provider to competitive tenders for training services
- Improved perception of managers from a sample of firms and business associations of: (i) relevance of training to employer needs, (ii) quality of training, and (iii) availability of potential employees with the needed skills.

Source: Adapted from R. Almeida, J. Behrman, and D. Robalino, eds. 2012. *The Right Skills for the Job? Rethinking Training Policies for Workers.* Washington, DC: World Bank; World Bank staff.
Note: NGO = nongovernmental organization.

Environmental Benefits Statement

The World Bank is committed to reducing its environmental footprint. In support of this commitment, the Publishing and Knowledge Division leverages electronic publishing options and print-on-demand technology, which is located in regional hubs worldwide. Together, these initiatives enable print runs to be lowered and shipping distances decreased, resulting in reduced paper consumption, chemical use, greenhouse gas emissions, and waste.

The Publishing and Knowledge Division follows the recommended standards for paper use set by the Green Press Initiative. Whenever possible, books are printed on 50 percent to 100 percent postconsumer recycled paper, and at least 50 percent of the fiber in our book paper is either unbleached or bleached using Totally Chlorine Free (TCF), Processed Chlorine Free (PCF), or Enhanced Elemental Chlorine Free (EECF) processes.

More information about the Bank's environmental philosophy can be found at http://crinfo.worldbank.org/wbcrinfo/node/4.

green
press
INITIATIVE